Leverage

Leverage

How Cheap Money Will Destroy the World

Karl Denninger

WILEY

John Wiley & Sons, Inc.

Published by John Wiley & Sons, Inc., Hoboken, New Jersey.
Published simultaneously in Canada.

For general information on our other products and services or for technical support, please contact our Customer Care Department within the United States at (800) 762-2974, outside the United States at (317) 572-3993 or fax (317) 572-4002.

Wiley also publishes its books in a variety of electronic formats. Some content that appears in print may not be available in electronic books. For more information about Wiley products, visit our web site at www.wiley.com.

Library of Congress Cataloging-in-Publication Data:

Denninger, Karl, 1963–
    Leverage: how cheap money will destroy the world / Karl Denninger.
      p. cm.
    Includes bibliographical references and index.
    ISBN 978-1-118-12284-6 (cloth); ISBN 978-1-118-16614-7 (ebk);
    ISBN 978-1-118-16615-4 (ebk); ISBN 978-1-118-16616-1 (ebk)
    1. Financial leverage. 2. Debt. I. Title.
    HG4521.D487 2012
    332–dc23

                                                        2011025473

ISBN 978-1-118-12284-6

Printed in the United States of America

10 9 8 7 6 5 4 3 2 1

Leverage is dedicated to my daughter Sarah, who will inherit the nation we leave her and her future family.

As we peer into society's future, we—you and I, and our government—must avoid the impulse to live only for today, plundering for our own ease and convenience the precious resources of tomorrow. We cannot mortgage the material assets of our grandchildren without risking the loss also of their political and spiritual heritage. We want democracy to survive for all generations to come, not to become the insolvent phantom of tomorrow.
—Dwight D. Eisenhower

Contents

Foreword

When you start experiencing severe chest pains, dizziness, and nausea, do you want the doctor to tell you, "Don't worry—you're fit as a fiddle, and everything's going to be fine"—or do you want the truth?

If you want a future, then you want the truth.

This is why Karl Denninger's *The Market Ticker* blog has long been a must-read for those who want a positive future for their children and their nation: he reports the truth.

The symptoms of systemic failure are painfully evident, but most Americans don't want to see the elephant sitting on the chest of the United States of America: leveraged debt, the so-called cheap money that will destroy our nation. Leveraged debt is crushing our households, enterprises, and government, yet such is the level of ignorance and fear that wishful thinking and false reassurances dominate the public dialogue.

The only way forward is to start with a truthful accounting of our financial illness, and that is precisely what this book serves up, with the same clear explanations and charts that have drawn those hungry for facts to Karl's blog.

If you want another serving of empty promises, media doublespeak, official obfuscation, or blatant self-interest masquerading as policy, you've come to the wrong place: Karl is absolutely fearless when dispatching the sacred cows that have gridlocked the national debate.

What you will get is a fact-based diagnosis of our ills and a non-ideological presentation of practical solutions. The goal here is nothing less than the restoration of the real economy over the financialized FIRE (finance, insurance, real estate) economy based on leveraged debt and a poisonous culture of fraud, embezzlement, collusion, and crony capitalism.

We seem to have lost our social and institutional memory of a healthy, transparent financial sector that doesn't rely on leverage, misrepresented risk, and bogus accounting to reap profits, and of a time when the financial sector did not dominate the real economy and the political process.

As Karl makes clear in these pages, the stakes couldn't be higher; the reliance on leverage has fatally undermined the U.S. economy, and the outsized political influence purchased by the financial sector's vast profiteering threatens our democracy.

This reliance on leverage and sleight-of-hand accounting has also undermined our ability to make fact-based assessments; rather than demand an honest appraisal that might threaten the status quo, we've allowed ourselves to be lulled into self-deceptive denial. This book is a wake-up call for everyone who puts their country and future generations of Americans ahead of their own self-interest.

In the public sphere, patriotism has been cheapened by an epidemic of single-minded self-interest to empty slogans and empty gestures, as if wearing an American flag lapel pin covered up the raw greed and self-interest behind the typical appeal to "the national interest." Karl challenges all Americans to examine the financial facts of the matter, and in so doing, set aside their own claims on future taxpayers in favor of fixing what's broken.

The great appeal of Karl's message is its depiction in simple-to-understand charts of our multiple financial illnesses, and its fearlessly direct appraisal of what we need to do to restore our economy and nation to health. Having a profoundly honest conversation about our ills and our options of treatment is the only way forward, and this book exemplifies the leadership we need: not the dishonest pandering of our political class, but instead speaking truthfully about the changes and sacrifices that must be made to restore the nation and its future. We don't have to agree on every point, but we do need to begin the conversation. This book shows us where to start.

Charles Hugh Smith
Author of *An Unconventional Guide to Investing
in Troubled Times* and www.oftwominds.com

Acknowledgments

I would like to thank the whole host of people without whom my drive to analyze the economic matters discussed here would not have been possible. Chief among them is my father, who was a CPA for a modest glass company during my youth and who both introduced me to the basics of bookkeeping and provided me with my first opportunity to program a computer for money at age 13. I doubt he had any idea where letting his son fix a tax table in an old bookkeeping machine would lead.

The early 2007 Asian market swoon deserves thanks for jolting me awake from what had been a very simple and profitable trading career for the previous four years. Also, the user community that developed around my web publication, *The Market Ticker,* provided encouragement for me to undertake the wider view of our economy and markets that you will find in these pages.

Finally, I'd like to thank both Janet Tavakoli, for her introduction to John Wiley & Sons, and the staff at Wiley themselves for their support in preparation and editing. Without them, *Leverage* would not have come to fruition.

Introduction

Leverage.

A simple word, really. When you use a bottle opener to uncap your favorite brew, you use leverage. When you pry open a can of paint with a screwdriver, you use leverage. And yet in the financial world, abuse of leverage has repeatedly led the economy to ruin.

Leverage is simply the trade-off of one element of motion or action for another. With the can of paint, your screwdriver has a quarter inch of movement at the business end under the lip, but four inches of movement on the handle. You thus multiply the force you exert by 16 times, but the trade-off is that the bit moves only a 16th as far.

With financial leverage, the same principle applies, except the trade-off is that losses multiply, exactly as do gains. Nearly everyone who undertakes a leveraged transaction understands this part of the essence of leverage.

But what's not thought about often is the inherent nature of leverage in the financial realm and how, as a consequence of the fundamentals of finance that go back over a thousand years, certain mathematical facts cannot be avoided.

It is, in fact, attempting to avoid the expression of these facts that leads to the worst financial panics and depressions.

It is my hope that this book will provide a unique perspective on these foundations of our financial life. None of this should need to be written down. These facts remain undiscussed in the financial media, and it would be fair to assume that even people like Federal Reserve Chairman Ben Bernanke don't understand the basic mathematics that underlay all financial systems.

Such an assumption would be terribly foolish, for it is only through the public's lack of knowledge that banking and financial interests can fleece our nation and, indeed, the people of all nations. If every American understood the facts I lay on the table in this book, there would have been no Internet bubble, no housing bubble, and no crisis of confidence in the financial system in 2008 and 2009.

What is discussed here is no less fundamental than the sun rising in the east each day and setting in the west. Without understanding these foundational principles, one cannot craft public policy to both accept what we cannot change and yet have outcomes that are acceptable for all actors in the financial system, both public and private.

One may argue with a mathematician, but one may not argue with the math itself.

Part One

LEVERAGE AND ITS ABUSES IN THE ECONOMY

Chapter 1

An Economic Future for America

Through the ages, the principle of financial leverage has been both used by the many and abused by the wealthy and powerful in society. The seduction of leverage is strong, in that it makes the difficult appear easy and the impossible seem to be within reach. It brings the illusion of equality between the wealthy man and the common laborer in the land of finance.

You can think of leverage as a drug, and an addictive one at that. Like many drugs, leverage is perfectly acceptable when used in moderation. But as with all addictive things, leverage has a lure that is indescribable once it is tasted. Who among us who has bought a house doesn't remember the first time we inserted the key in our new-to-us home and walked through the front door? The house is devoid of furniture and fashion, a box into which we would load our lives, and we quickly forget that we don't really own the house since a bank has the legal right to our title. The new car smell is likewise one that people consider a rite of passage, even though that smell is probably a derivative of formaldehyde and rather unhealthy!

The seduction of having a little plastic card in your wallet that can buy the equivalent of a car in seconds with no money in the bank is powerful. Many have walked into a shopping mall and an hour or two later emerged with thousands of dollars' worth of clothing, jewelry, perfumes, and baubles that they have no idea how they're going to pay for. Indeed, how many of us didn't chuckle to some degree at the comedy *Confessions of a Shopaholic* on the silver screen and failed to identify, in some small way, with the pithy phrase "Really declined."

In the financial panic of 2007 to 2009, who could fail to note that certain wealthy and powerful people seem to have not only escaped the wrath of contraction in the economy and credit but also profited tremendously from these events? Others of apparent wealth and many of modest means have been rendered destitute. Millions of jobs disappeared, salaries and wages were slashed, and as of early 2011, more than a million homes have been lost to foreclosure.

Some have put forward the theory that certain people of money and influence have the ability to sway events to their liking through various forms of bribery, whether legal or not, with regulators and members of government. Still others believe that luck is responsible for the difference in outcomes. Neither view is correct.

Some wealthy people do indeed use their influence with government officials and even resort to actions that could be called extortion when the economy turns downward. Influence peddling, bribery, and threats are as old as politics itself, and it should not surprise anyone that the rich and powerful are at the center of these activities when their wealth is threatened.

To stop the abuses of leverage in our financial markets, we must first identify the fundamental nature of leverage and how structures are set up to disadvantage the general public. The abuse of these structures requires that the average person be ignorant of the fundamental nature of capital. They must not understand how capital and leverage, otherwise known as debt, are fungible, and how certain mathematical facts guarantee outcomes over time in the economy as a whole. This lack of knowledge among the populace is then exploited by the few in positions of power to set up edifices that strip the general population of their wealth, much like a whale is flensed after being harpooned, leaving the public in debt peonage. Eventually these artificial structures always collapse, exactly as they did during the California Gold Rush. The collapse leaves wealthy only those who exploited the bubble to skim off a piece of the activity via selling blue jeans, picks, and shovels, while the majority of others who engaged in the Ponzi scheme are bereft of both a job and their allegedly accumulated wealth.

Only through an understanding of history, along with the fundamental nature of leverage in the economy, can we change the economic system to end these abuses. While there are many who argue that the market is efficient and left to its own devices will govern these matters on its own, the presence of governments and thus the inevitable corruption that comes with them makes this option entirely unsatisfactory. There are choices available to us, and we as a body politic can choose to demand their implementation.

Should we fail to address these imbalances, there will be dire consequences for the United States and indeed the entire world economic system. We can no longer pretend that the Federal Reserve holds the power to address what's wrong with an economy that is structurally defective, just as we cannot fix a collapsing bridge by painting new lines to divide the lanes of traffic and claim that the structure has been rehabilitated.

■　■　■

Consider America's future, where your children and grandchildren will live their lives. What will it look like from an economic perspective?

If you look at the U.S. labor market today, you see more than 30 years of exporting manufacturing jobs overseas. The first exodus was to Japan, which destroyed the U.S. television and automobile industries. The second was to China, which destroyed large swaths of high-tech manufacturing and assembly. While the United States has maintained manufacturing output, it has come almost exclusively through mechanization and productivity gains; manufacturing employment has plunged by half since 1979 and stands at roughly 11.5 million as of March 2011, despite the population increasing by almost 50 percent during the same time period.[1] The alleged economic recovery from 2009 onward has come with more than three-quarters of all the jobs created paying below $15 an hour, well under the national average hourly wage of $22.50.

In 2011, we have crushing levels of federal, state, and local debt, and more than a third of all so-called wage income is paid by some form of entitlement program, whether it be Social Security, welfare, Section 8 housing, or food stamps. One in six households cannot afford to buy food in America, a 58 percent increase in three years' time.[2] Our civilian population employment rate, the percentage of adults who are in the workforce, is back to where it was before women joined the workforce en masse in the 1970s. Contrary to economic projections in 2000 that the federal government would be debt-free by 2010, our federal debt more than doubled from $5.7 trillion to nearly $15 trillion, and the unfunded mandates in Social Security, Medicare, and Medicaid total approximately $100 trillion. Our total indebtedness and obligations are roughly seven times the total economic output of the United States. In April 2011, Secretary of the Treasury Timothy Geithner threatened to raid federal employee retirement funds if Congress refused to allow the Treasury to borrow even more money.[3]

The future one can see ahead on the path we currently walk is bleak.

What if you were to learn that there is a path forward that will produce a better tomorrow? Would you insist on changes today that would bring prosperity back to the United States, even if those changes would produce severe short-term economic discomfort?

We can have a nation and economy that manufactures most of what we consume at home. The United States can have abundant and stable energy supplies. We can have a stable, sound banking system that matches lenders and borrowers, along with clearing payments, but does not encourage speculation. We can have sound money with no inflation over decades-long periods of time. We can have a college system where your children can afford to put themselves through school working part-time, taking on no debt, with only a small contribution from you as their parents. And we can have medical care that delivers excellent outcomes without bankrupting you, your employer, and our society as a whole.

With a labor force that is vibrant and earns wages in the United States producing cars, televisions, computers, and more, our middle class can afford to buy the goods and services they produce. Credit will be uncommonly used in the population, reserved for true emergencies and extraordinary events instead of being a staple of everyday life. Interest payments will be small and uncommon. Speculators will be free to place their bets, but they won't be able to demand handouts when they lose in the Wall Street casino. You will be able to save 10 percent of your gross income during your working years and, coupled with a Social Security system that remains solvent, live out your life without having to speculate in the stock market. A house will be a place where you hang your hat instead of a get-rich-quick scheme that blows up in your face and results in foreclosure, eviction, and financial destitution.

Some Americans will choose to start businesses and employ others. Those who do will not fear having their product's design ripped off in China and sold without compensation or fear that their competitor will utilize slave labor and environmental pollution as a strategy to put them out of business. The rest of the United States, who work for someone else, will compete against other first-world nations and their citizens for jobs rather than against near-literal slave labor being paid $2 a day.

■   ■   ■

We hear constantly about income inequality in the United States, but there are two forms of income inequality, and one of them is positive for the nation. The rich person who becomes wealthy by inventing a new process or widget brings wealth to everyone. Henry Ford made possible ownership of an automobile by virtually every man who worked for him on the assembly line. To deny him the wealth that flowed from his innovation would be to prevent the production of the Model T, and America would have been much poorer. But some people become wealthy by finding ways to effectively screw the public, putting in place legal and business systems that skim off funds without providing anything of real value in return. Our focus should be not on flattening income inequality but rather on getting rid of the economic and legal structures that allow and protect theft while encouraging competition and entrepreneurship. We should encourage many Henry Fords and Thomas Edisons in our society rather than those who use financial trickery as a means of enriching themselves at the expense of the public.

Tax systems that are designed for social agendas provide a convenient foil for those who would demagogue political issues for their own ends, and the United States suffers greatly for it. Our tax code has become part of an intentionally convoluted economic structure that is designed to consign the common man to debt peonage and poverty. Why else would we tax long-term capital gains, the fruit of a successful investment that employs others, while at the same time allowing a tax deduction for interest on consumed capital goods, particularly housing, which can only make you poorer?

The United States emerged from World War II as an economic powerhouse unequaled before in the world. Where we produced tanks and aircraft for war, we turned to peaceful production of automobiles and airliners. Where we produced radar screens, we changed those factories over to produce televisions. Where we produced nuclear weapons that ended the war, we turned our ability toward peaceful nuclear power and currently obtain 20 percent of our electricity from exploitation of the atom.

We can return to our former status as an economic powerhouse without equal. America lost its way not because there are other nations with a better political structure, a smarter population, or more resources than we possess. We stumbled and fell through a common path of corruption called leverage that has played out time and time again through history. The salve found in leverage is much like alcohol; the first drink does no harm and makes you feel good. The tenth has you in the bathroom hugging porcelain. If you do not learn from your mistakes and continue to increase your consumption, rather than choosing to be a teetotaler, you will eventually suffer liver cancer or alcohol poisoning and die.

■   ■   ■

You have taken the first step on the path of understanding how the United States, like so many other nations, lost its way. But unlike many other books through the years, here you will also find how we can regain the path of prosperity.

The choices before us are not simple ones, but they are necessary. Our path toward destruction did not happen in an afternoon, a month, or a year. We have been destroying our nation through debt alcoholism for more than three decades, and recovery will take time. There will be setbacks and pain, as there always is when breaking an addiction. Our focus as a nation must be not on the binge of today but rather on how we sustain our economy and people through both today's generation and tomorrow's.

Every journey to set right what has been wrong begins with a first step. Before we embark on our journey of reconstruction, we must understand how we both broke our nation and became broke so we can avoid the traps that were intentionally set by those who corrupted our future. Without understanding the foibles of the past, we have no hope of avoiding them tomorrow. Those who profit mightily from the current economic structure in which we find ourselves trapped will not easily give up the privilege they have won through decades of trickery and deceit. It is only through understanding why the alleged solutions they put forward cannot work that we, the people of this nation, can challenge and depose their bankrupt economic prescriptions, replacing them with sound alternatives.

America's future down one road is dark and foreboding, while down the other, it is vibrant and exciting. We stand at a fork in the road, and our challenge is to choose the path that looks rockier at the outset, but leads onward and upward toward sunshine and a warm summer's breeze rather than downward to ruin.

Chapter 2

Principles of
Financial Leverage

C apital and leverage are inextricably intertwined. *Capital* is a single word that denotes the fruits of one's labor that have been reduced into an easily exchanged form and frequently manifests in what we call money. Idle capital is a mere store of wealth, but when put to work, it builds businesses, employs workers, and generates productivity throughout the economy.

Leverage is simply the use of debt to replace capital in a transaction. Both leverage and capital spend in the economy in exactly the same way, just as a credit card in your wallet spends exactly the same as does a $20 bill. When it is recognized as the functional equivalent of capital, it is easy to see how leverage can become addictive, as it allows a person, corporation, or government to act as if they have amassed much capital, when in fact they have little or none at all.

In the general sense, there are four types of capital utilization that can be undertaken in the economy. Three of them are conveniently called investments. The four categories of capital utilization and the relative risk involved in using leverage to replace the capital used are:

1. **Productive Investment.** This is best exemplified by the purchase of a machine that makes widgets, which are then sold to customers. The machine has a cost, and with the input of raw materials, labor, and energy, that machine produces an output that the investor hopes has more value in the marketplace than the sum of the input costs. Combined with adroit management and utilization, use of capital in this manner produces a net positive return to the economy as a whole. The risk of loss lies in the miscalculation of the final value of the products or services produced by the machine, in that there is never a guarantee that whatever comes out of the machine will sell for more than the sum of the expenses. This use of capital is routinely able to be profitably financed using leverage for both the borrower and lender.

2. **Speculative Investment.** This is best exemplified by the direct purchase at an initial public offering (IPO) or other direct offering of capital stock in a corporation that produces goods or services. Such a company must, of course, be able to produce a positive cash flow against operating expenses, including debt service. The use of capital *itself* produces no inherent return; however, through the exploitation of the capital gained by the seller of the investment, a net positive rate of return can be obtained. The level of indirection—that is, reliance on a third party for performance and the possibility that the borrower will spend the funds instead of productively investing them—inherently increases the risk involved in using one's capital in this fashion. This type of capital use, when financed through leverage in whole or part, is potentially dangerous because the carrying cost of the debt is additive to the acquisition expense, and the investor lacks direct control over the ultimate use of the borrowed funds.

3. **Consumption.** This category, as opposed to the others, is not thought of as an investment at all but rather is the dissipation of capital for the purpose of enjoyment of one's life. Some of the consumption we undertake is involuntary; our basic needs such as food and some degree of clothing and energy use are physical

necessities of life without which we will literally expire. Housing properly falls into this category; but in the 2000s, housing was moved downward one step with disastrous results. When viewed as a durable good, housing, like transportation, is thought of as an item that has declining natural value due to its maintenance expense. This use of capital is dangerous to engage in using leverage because in addition to pulling forward tomorrow's demand into today, you are adding the financing cost to the total price you will pay, and the asset in question is ultimately consumed.

4. **Ponzi scheme.** A use of capital is properly considered a Ponzi scheme if the only way the purchased item can increase in value is by locating someone who will pay a higher price. While Ponzi schemes are often called investments, they in fact never are. Housing is one such category when viewed not as a place to live in or rent out to someone else but rather as an item you acquire for capital appreciation. To generate continual growth of such an asset's value, either you must generate continually advancing demand or you must find some way to make purchasing your asset easier so as to be able to justify a higher price. The same principle holds true for the purchase of stock on an exchange for capital appreciation rather than dividend income. This use of capital is inherently unstable and, when compound growth occurs, poses extreme risk of eventual price collapse when the next buyer fails to materialize. *Leverage, otherwise known as debt, should never be used to buy into any Ponzi scheme.* If your timing is wrong and the next sucker fails to appear, the leverage you have taken on is immediately exposed. The risk of bankruptcy in such a situation is extremely high since not only can you lose your original investment but also the borrowed funds may be lost.

Economic panics and depressions throughout history have typically been generated as a direct consequence of people shifting their use of leverage toward consumption and Ponzi schemes to a greater and greater degree, and away from productive investment. As these shifts begin, the illusion of free money becomes common in the general population. Stories are printed in the media and circulate around the dinner table of persons who have put in little or no capital of their own yet are living like kings and enjoying the trappings of luxury, all by borrowing to allegedly invest.

The seduction of inexpensive debt and the apparent riches that can be skimmed off through its use is difficult to resist. The earliest recorded bubble in common literature is probably the tulip mania[1] that took place during 1636 and 1637 in Holland. The price of various exotic tulip bulbs underwent a more than 20:1 increase over the space of just a few months, although few if any actual deliveries of bulbs took place. Instead, the Dutch traded contracts remarkably similar to our modern-day futures in that they allowed one to purchase a bulb today for delivery at a future date, paying only a small transaction fee. There were no margin requirements or any supervision of the ability to pay the full contracted price, however, and as a result, only through finding another purported investor willing to buy your contract could you turn your paper contractual gain into actual money.

When the price of tulips collapsed in the early months of 1637, those who held the contracts were left with an obligation to buy a bulb at many times its current market value. The government responded to the incipient destruction of many people's wealth by changing the law in February 1637, allowing those who were stuck with these contracts to get out of them by paying a small penalty. Tulip mania is thus not only the first speculative bubble but also the first recorded bailout for those who got caught up in a Ponzi scheme and would have otherwise been financially ruined.

Following the U.S. Civil War, there was a boom in railroad construction. More than 50,000 miles of track were laid between 1866 and 1873, enabled by government land grants. Speculative capital underlay much of the construction, even though at the time there was no proven demand for the rail lines that were to operate once the track was finished. Modern finance and computers did not exist, of course, but traditional bond-style funding was plentiful and inexpensive. A huge number of bond issues were sold to the public not only for the construction of railroads themselves but also to finance construction of ports, stations, and terminals associated with the new rail lines. These new rail lines and associated projects had been funded not with saved capital but rather with what looked at the time to be extremely cheap debt, as the expected profits to be earned by these rail lines danced in investors' imaginations. Mechanization of U.S. farms following the Civil War also contributed to the boom, as the cost of farming in the United States fell more rapidly than in Europe, making U.S. farm products more competitive in European nations.

In 1871, Germany decided to move away from its use of silver as a monetary metal. This depressed demand for silver, much of which was mined in the western United States to which these rail lines had been extended. The United States responded to falling silver demand by dropping its silver coinage backing as well, moving to an effective gold-only monetary standard in 1873 through the Coinage Act.[2] The impact of this law was dramatic in that in addition to causing the price of silver to drop further, it called into question the stability of U.S. monetary policy. Longer-term bond obligations fell into immediate disfavor, as inexpensive long-term bond financing is inextricably tied to the expectation of stable monetary value. Being a highly durable sort of investment, railroad bonds had typically been of long duration, and many investors had borrowed to purchase them. The value of their holdings declined precipitously, calling into question their solvency. Jay Cook and Company, a major banking interest that was funding what was to become the Northern Pacific Railway, failed to close on a $300 million government loan after reports circulated that their credit was exhausted due to the decline in long-duration bond values. The firm collapsed.

A chain-reaction set of bank failures followed, and the New York Stock Exchange was closed for 10 days to attempt to sort out the mess left by companies that suddenly found themselves with rapidly deteriorating bond positions that they had counted as allegedly safe capital. The speculative mania that had driven the issuance of debt for the funding of these railroads collapsed with dramatic force, and layoffs rippled through factories and rail lines. Unemployment reached 14 percent, and a quarter of the nation's railroads went bankrupt over the next three years. Subsequent strikes by railroad labor unions in 1877 to protest layoffs and falling wages led President Hayes to send federal troops in an attempt to break the strikes. More than 100 strikers were killed in the skirmishes that followed.

The Panic of 1873 required six years of deflation and debt destruction before the financial imbalances that had been built up in the previous seven years were cleared from the economy. [3]

Everyone has read about the 1929 stock market crash and the Roaring Twenties. What's not commonly written about is what made the 1920s roar. It was cheap leverage, or debt, that was once again behind the speculative craze. In addition to a wave of industrialization and advances in technology, the first use of leverage to buy household appliances and homes was thrust into the mainstream. Land speculation with risky mortgages was rampant, especially in Florida. As prices rapidly increased, the balloon mortgage, where one paid only interest on the loan for a period of a few years, with the entire principal due at the end of the term, became the primary means of real estate purchase nationwide. Stocks were bought with leverage as well, with brokerage houses allowing the purchase of $10 worth of stock with only $1 of actual capital on deposit. The Dow Jones stock index rose from 64 in 1921 to a high of 383 in 1929, a nearly 500 percent increase in eight years.

Those who were paying attention noticed in late 1925 that land prices in Florida had stopped rising. A few newspapers and magazines ran articles warning that prices were being driven solely by the expectation of finding a buyer at a higher price. Panic quickly set in, as speculators who had bought property with nothing more than a letter of credit began to have trouble finding new buyers and were called on to perform on loans they never believed they would have to pay. A pair of hurricanes in 1926 and 1928 destroyed infrastructure in the southern half of the state and left the Florida property market in ruins, but most investors believed the property collapse was local to the state and was not a consequence of severe economic imbalances that had become embedded throughout the nation. They were wrong.

From 1927 onward, arguably in an attempt to blunt the impact of the Florida property collapse, pundits and politicians made statements that were later proved wildly inaccurate. It can be argued that these statements were nothing more than intentional attempts to keep confidence high on what was known to be a bubble about to burst. Among them were the following quotes from people of particular note:

We will not have any more crashes in our time.
                              —John Maynard Keynes in 1927

There may be a recession in stock prices, but not anything in the nature
of a crash.
                              —Irving Fisher, leading U.S. economist,
                              New York Times, September 5, 1929

The October 1929 stock market crash brought into stark relief the
folly of leveraged speculation. With only 10 percent down required by
brokers, the crash destroyed many investors overnight as their margin
was immediately wiped out. The paper gains they had been counting
as real wealth evaporated, and the resulting margin calls could not be
met. Homes and land that had been purchased on balloon notes with
the expectation that a refinance would always be possible were lost to
foreclosure as the value of property fell and the owner could not make
the balloon payment or refinance into another product. The government attempted to stem the liquidation of massive bad debt with both
direct action and speeches that cast the economic future in a favorable
light, including statements like the following:

This crash is not going to have much effect on business.
                              —Arthur Reynolds, Chairman of
                              Continental Illinois Bank of
                              Chicago, October 24, 1929

I see nothing in the present situation that is either menacing or warrants
pessimism. . . . I have every confidence that there will be a revival of
activity in the spring, and that during this coming year the country will
make steady progress.
                              —Andrew W. Mellon, U.S. Secretary
                              of the Treasury, December 31, 1929

I am convinced that through these measures we have reestablished
confidence.
                              —President Herbert Hoover, December 1929

Nothing of the sort, of course, was true.

The Great Depression was only great due to its length; from a
standpoint of economic contraction in a brief period of time, both
the 1873 and 1920 downturns were far more violent. Ending only

when the United States entered World War II, the Great Depression featured forced currency devaluation, the establishment of an artificial market for home loans in the form of Fannie Mae,[4] confiscation of privately held gold,[5] the intentional destruction of crops by the Roosevelt administration in an attempt to prevent crop price deflation,[6] and more. All were attempts to prevent the market from clearing out speculative excess that had been embedded in the form of leverage, and all were unsuccessful for the simple fact that the economy had built into itself levels of production for which there was no demand that could be paid for with current output. When the pyramid of leverage collapsed, there was nobody to buy these products and services, businesses were bankrupted, and unemployment became rampant.

The standard of living to which the people had been accustomed had not been bought with personal output in the economy but rather had been paid for with borrowing. Stripped of the ability to continue to pile leverage upon leverage, the government was faced with the choice of either allowing all of the Ponzi schemes to collapse of their own weight or attempt to salvage some of them. Both Herbert Hoover and Franklin D. Roosevelt chose the latter path, and despite unprecedented intervention, neither administration was successful. It was only the demand surge that came from wartime production and the concurrent destruction of virtually all industrial capacity in Europe during World War II that raised economic demand after the war and finally allowed the economy to truly recover.

The Great Depression, however, did bring about one positive change. There was an investigation of the root causes of the collapse that was ultimately called the Pecora Commission. Hearings began in early 1932, but due to political infighting, three chairmen resigned in disgust. Ferdinand Pecora was subsequently hired to write the final report and discovered that the information necessary to do so was incomplete. He asked for and was granted subpoena power; the subsequent hearings ran until 1934 with the final report leading to the birth of the Securities and Exchange Commission (SEC).

Concurrently with the latter part of these hearings, the Banking Act of 1933 was passed, otherwise known as Glass–Steagall.[7] Congress found that part of the cause of unsound leverage in the economy prior to the 1929 crash and depression was the comingling of commercial banking activities funded by depositors and securities transactions, such as underwriting and trading stocks and bonds. When securities prices collapsed, commercial banks, which had been extending loans against their deposits for this leveraged activity, became immediately insolvent. Glass-Steagall separated investment and commercial banking and prohibited commercial banks from dealing in securities or insurance products, effectively sheltering depositor funds from being lent out for speculative activity. Investment banks were prohibited depositors, forcing them to obtain their capital via bonds or stockholders, an effective loan to the bank by investors concurrent with the risk of loss.

Glass-Steagall, while not perfect, stands as one of the most effective laws of all time in terms of controlling systemic risk and excessive economic leverage. It was not until 1984, 50 years later, that we would have a bank be deemed too big to fail and thus require financial intervention in the form of a bailout. Much of the law's success undoubtedly came from its brevity; it is awfully difficult to find loopholes in a law that is entirely encompassed within 17 pages.

With this long history of economic panics and depressions, one must ask why the same economic outcomes repeatedly develop, despite often-repeated claims that we have become smarter or more knowledgeable over time. The answer is the fundamental behavior of leverage in an economy. Leverage, when utilized, always obeys certain fundamental mathematical laws, and it is only through the willful refusal to allow these mathematical laws to contain excessive use of leverage that systemically important manias can develop. To bring the long parade of bubbles under control, along with understanding why Glass-Steagall resulted in nearly 50 years of comparative stability, we must begin by examining these fundamental relationships.

■ ■ ■

The basics of finance are taught in home economics courses in high schools across the land. Each year millions of our youth are shown how a checkbook works, along with the importance of balancing that checkbook. Some of those students are fortunate enough to be shown how to run a household budget and divide household spending into expenses that must be paid and expenses that can be deferred or avoided.

We're also taught the basics of buying something on time. When we pay over time, we are introduced to paying interest. Some teachers and instructors go over a basic amortization table, and if you did really well in choosing your school, you'll have explained to you that if you buy a house with a 30-year mortgage, you'll typically pay for the house twice, due to those pesky and unavoidable interest charges.

These basic lessons are fine as far as they go. But it is the omission of two fundamental facts and how they interact that do the real harm to financial understanding by the public. Specifically:

1. Nobody ever lends anyone money at an intentional loss.
2. Due to the mathematical essence of exponents, two compound growth functions, such as growth in GDP and borrowing that must be paid for with that GDP, will *always* run away from each other over time.

Contemplate these two basic principles for a moment, and you may begin to understand the basics of the business cycle and why throughout history there have always been ups and downs in the economy.

We often hear that businesses hire too many people and produce too many things when times are good because they miscalculate the future prospects for their businesses. That is, businesspeople tend to be irrational and that irrationality produces inevitable business cycles. This is incorrect. *Business cycles occur because of the immutable laws of mathematics.*

The first and most important is the basic premise of exponents. We all hear talk of 3 percent growth or 2 percent inflation in the financial media. What the speaker is referring to is a compound function, that is, 103 percent of something this year as compared to last year. Growth sounds innocent enough when spoken of in this fashion. How can a 2, 3, or 5 percent increase in something harm you?

Over the short term it doesn't. It's the long term that's the problem, as illustrated in Figure 2.1.

That graph looks somewhat ugly or somewhat good, depending on your point of view: $1,000 that grows at 5 percent a year in 30 years is $4,321 and change. That's more than four times the money

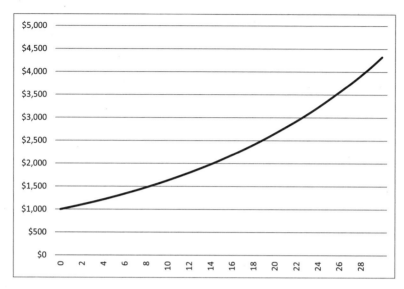

Figure 2.1   5 Percent Growth of $1,000 over 30 Years

you started with over 30 years. The time to double for a compound function is such a common computation that there's a rule for it called the rule of 72. The rule states that the amount of time in years that something takes to double is approximated by dividing 72 by the growth or interest rate. If we take 72 and divide it by 5, you will see that the rule is approximately correct in that $1,000 turns into $2,000 in about 14 years.

If you're detecting the start of something bad in this formula, however, you're right. Figure 2.2 shows what the same chart looks like with a 100-year timeline.

Best of luck to you in making that work out. Your $1,000 turns into more than $120,000 over that 100-year period. This is the often-repeated magic of compound earnings that various commentators cite as the miracle enabling you to invest in even mediocre growth stocks and bonds while turning a handsome profit. The commentators are right, but they are telling you only half the truth, and the other half is just as ugly as this is beautiful. Somehow that $120,000 will have to be found to pay you with. The money to pay that debt, in short, has to come from somewhere.

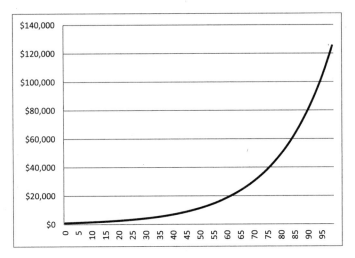

Figure 2.2   5 Percent Growth over 100 Years

The larger problem arrives when you have two of these compound functions, one with a larger percentage of growth than the other. The key to remember in finance is that this is *always* going to be true. Everyone in an economic system seeks to earn a positive return over time. As such, they always seek to charge more than their costs, whether those costs come from manufacturing something or lending money.

Figure 2.3 illustrates the problem, starting with a $1,000 amount.

These numbers, 4 percent growth in output and 7 percent growth in debt, were not picked arbitrarily. They approximate the difference between growth in GDP, that is, growth in the economy, and growth in debt since the early 1950s when the Fed started issuing a quarterly statistical report called the Z1.[8]

As you can see, these two curves representing the output of the economy and the amount of debt that the economy has in it inevitably run away from one other. This process is governed by the laws of mathematics. The key to understanding Figure 2.3 is that this outcome always occurs whenever you have two compound functions where one element grows at a rate faster than the other. It cannot be avoided, whether by government declaration or by innovation in financial products. The inevitable result is as immutable as is the fact that $2 + 2 = 4$.

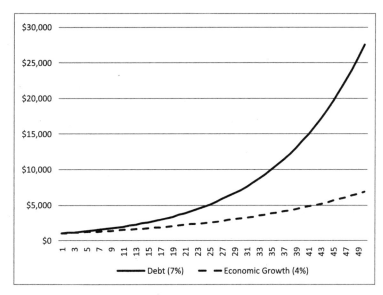

Figure 2.3   Growth and Debt over 50 Years

Now let's look at another unfortunate fact. We'll assume the debt in question carries interest at 6 percent. What happens to your cash flow, that is, the amount of money you have after you pay the interest due from your growing earnings through economic progress? Figure 2.4 tells the story.

That doesn't look so bad. But take note that your debt service has slowly started eating into your earnings. At the beginning of this process, the required debt service, or interest, is just $60, or 6 percent of your $1,000 in earnings. But by the 50th year it's $1,651.80 out of $6,833.33, or 24 percent of your earnings. That's four times as much in percentage terms.

You might think you can handle these figures, but it should be obvious what's going to happen if you keep on this path in growing your debt and income. In 100 years, the chart looks like Figure 2.5.

The bad news is that you owe more than $800,000, starting with a mere $1,000 in debt. The worse news is that you make only $48,562.45 and the interest payments are $48,656.99. It has become impossible to pay off the debt because the interest payments exceed your income, leaving you nothing with which to reduce the principal.

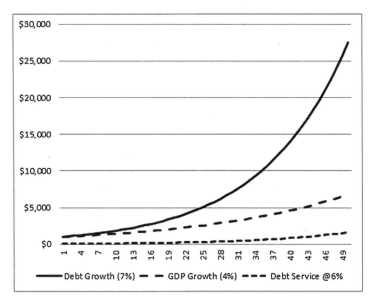

Figure 2.4   Growth, Debt, and Debt Service

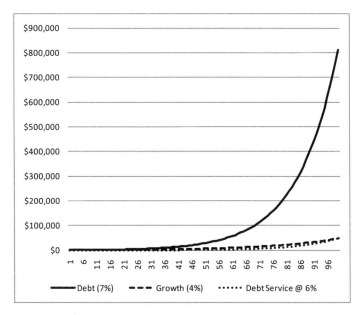

Figure 2.5   Growth, Debt, and Interest in 100 Years

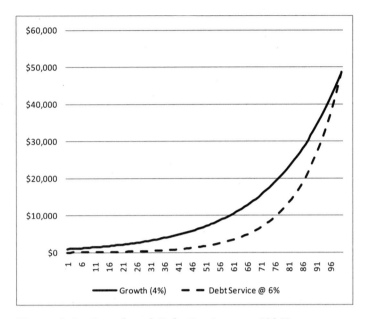

Figure 2.6 Growth and Debt Service over 100 Years

It's easier to see what happens to you if we remove the top line, showing only your income and the debt service on the debt. See Figure 2.6.

The seduction to begin deficit spending, whether as an individual or a government, is in the first years. The belly of Figure 2.6 looks very manageable for quite a while, even though as a percentage of income, your debt service requirement is rising each and every year, eroding the amount of money that can be spent on other purchases. Interest payments look reasonable at the outset, and of course, the claim is always made that accumulating debt can stop in the next year, just like an alcoholic can stop drinking tomorrow. But then tomorrow comes, and the need to continue deficit spending to keep funding our lifestyles and entitlements has not abated. Soon people begin sounding the alarm, claiming that the path we are on is unsustainable. Still, the numbers look manageable at that moment in time, and so we kick the can some more.

Remember from your home economics class that not all the income you see on the chart is yours to spend. You must pay taxes as

an individual, along with paying for housing and food, and governments have what they call mandatory spending. For governments,
mandatory spending is made up of political promises made to certain
groups, otherwise called entitlements. Cutting entitlements inevitably
leads to the wrath of the voters and frequently the loss of a legislator's
job. As a result of the necessary expenditures, the crossover point where
the government or an individual cannot pay the interest owed, or
is forced to reduce mandatory spending, comes far before the theoretical limit.

The truly ugly part of the mathematics in these self-imposed hells
is the action you must take to get out of the hole. Assuming you
recognize the danger before you go bankrupt, you must cut back by
more than the amount of the excess spending you have been funding
with debt. In our examples, we are attempting to finance our profli-
gacy by increasing the amount of debt we carry by 3 percent more
than our income (or productive output) increases. That is, we're trying
to turn a 4 percent economic increase into a 7 percent one. To reverse
course, we not only must meet all the debt service with our cash flow
but also must reduce our spending by more than the 3 percent difference. Cutting spending by less than 3 percent increases the amount
of time we have before we inevitably go bankrupt, but it cannot
change the outcome. Only through actually paying down the debt's
principal can we retreat from the abyss.

Unfortunately, the longer you wait to address this problem, the
worse it becomes, as the interest payment continues to rise, compelling
you to attempt borrowing even more just to keep up with the interest
expense, much less your advance in alleged growth.

The bad news when it comes to breaking a debt cycle is not
limited to the simple mathematical relationships that govern it. Those
relationships set a minimum reduction in spending but not a practical
one, as yet another unfortunate reality impairing our ability to pay
down debt is present in all economic systems.

■　■　■

If you've had any sort of formal education in physics, even in high
school, you're aware of the laws of thermodynamics. In brief, they state

that all use of energy is subject to unavoidable loss. That is, all physical processes involving energy are in fact negative-sum games. This principle applies to economics as well, and the failure to recognize and account for it is one of the major failures among professional economists.

Anyone who has ever traded stocks, bonds, futures, or options, however, knows the negative sum of the market is true, just as it is true if you go to Las Vegas and play poker. You would expect at the poker table that if you win, the other players, in combination, must lose, and if the game is held at your home around the kitchen table, you're correct. But this is not true in a professional setting. At the poker table in Vegas, the loss comes in the form of the house rake, the percentage of the pot that is taken by the house for the privilege of playing poker. If you and six of your friends sit at such a table, and everyone is of equal skill and has an equal amount of luck in the cards they draw, eventually all of you will wind up with no money. It is a mathematical certainty if you play long enough, because in each hand you play, the house takes its cut. To win, you must not only be better than the other players but also be better by a high enough percentage or be lucky enough that you can overcome the house's rake, and you must stop playing and cash in your winnings before you inevitably donate all of your money to the house's drop box.

In financial markets, the same thing happens. When you buy or sell a stock, the brokerage takes the spread between the seller and buyer. This spread is often very small, but it is not zero. In addition, there is a fee charged for the trade both by the exchange and by your broker to handle the transaction. Therefore, to win, you not only must be better than the other party but also must be of superior knowledge and intellect by enough to overcome the rake that is imposed on your transactions.

At the store, the rake takes the form of a sales tax, along with other taxes and fees that are imposed by governments during the steps of production. In some nations, this tax is explicit, such as in Europe, where they have a value added tax (VAT) imposed on the value added in each step of production, from raw materials to the final sale. In the United States, this tax is implicit, in that each entity that handles a good or service from its origin to final sale is required to fund taxes paid out of their operations.

In point of fact, all transactions in an economy have loss to the participants. A third party always obtains the benefit of that loss, just as the energy you expel out the tailpipe of your car doesn't do you a bit of good in propelling you down the highway. The more transparency one has and the more participants there are in a market, the lower this loss is, but it is never zero. The funds that governments collect in taxes are also subject to inefficiency and corruption.

In addition, humans are imperfect beings. We make mistakes on a frequent basis, and this adds to loss because it leads us to enter into transactions where there is little or no actual benefit to us. As one example, we often discard items that still have utility value, destroying the remaining value of an asset on purpose. A teardown house where the home is inhabitable is one such example. On occasion, government steps in and adds to this loss, such as what happened with cash for clunkers,[9] where perfectly serviceable cars were taken off the road and intentionally destroyed in an attempt to drive the sale of new cars. While cash for clunkers undoubtedly caused new car sales to increase, it also removed from the market serviceable vehicles that people with few funds could buy, thereby driving up the cost of used vehicles, along with destroying the engines in traded cars that could have been used to repair older vehicles. This increase in used car prices, in turn, caused those individuals to spend more money than they otherwise would have on acquiring basic transportation. In the cash for clunkers case, there was essentially no analysis performed to quantify the negative economic impact on those of lesser means from the destruction of these vehicles. Government and private analysis was all focused on the benefit to the auto industry. Perhaps it was of benefit for the carmakers, but the costs of the program were much higher than admitted to; those costs included not only the tax money that went to the buyers but also the increased economic expense that those who would have normally driven and acquired the destroyed vehicles had forced upon them. In the particular case of cash for clunkers, the people who were hurt the most were also those least able to pay, the working poor and young adults.

Economists tend to ignore these measures of loss in their models and calculations, but they are always present. Embedded and unrecognized loss, along with the fact that all parties to a transaction will seek to earn a profit, is one of the fundamental features that drive separation in the compound functions that underlay long-run difficulties we have with growth and debt in the economy. The next time you hear someone touting a government program to create demand or motivate someone to engage in economic activity, the proper response is to ask them to identify all the hidden costs in that alleged beneficial program, including the ones that are imposed on third parties against their will.

■   ■   ■

If you follow the financial media, you have probably heard the term *naked shorting*. To short a stock, you sell the firm's stock without owning it first, and then if the price declines, you buy the stock back and keep the difference between your sale and purchase. This is one of the ways in which someone who has a negative view on a company can attempt to capitalize on their belief that the stock price will decline.

There's one problem with this general concept: How can you sell something you don't own? To solve this dilemma in the stock-trading world, legitimate short sales are conducted by borrowing the shares from someone else. That is, if you want to short 100 shares of IBM, you first must find someone who owns 100 shares of IBM stock and convince them to let you borrow their IBM shares. You then give the owner of the IBM shares an IOU for the 100 shares and sell the shares you have borrowed into the market.

There are now 100 more shares of stock circulating than there should be, because the original person who owned the stock had no intention to sell. That excess circulation is balanced by the IOU, which is enforceable against the person who borrowed the stock. If the person holding the IOU wishes to sell the stock at any point, the short-seller must return the borrowed shares so the owner can do so. The short-seller who cannot find someone else to borrow shares from is then forced to buy the stock to return his borrowed shares to their owner at whatever the current price for that stock may be. This sometimes forces the short-seller to take a heavy loss.

Naked shorting occurs when you sell stock short *without* securing the loan of the stock first. That is, you simply sell shares you don't have. This results in what is called a fail to deliver, because the person you sell stock to is entitled to actual shares of stock, and three trading days after you sell those shares, you have to settle the trade. If you can't deliver the shares for any reason, that position is called a naked short.

Naked short sales are illegal, with limited exceptions, for two reasons. First, they are the sale of something you do not possess, exactly as if you agreed to sell a Cadillac without having one and then took the purchaser's money for the car. If you are then unable to deliver the Cadillac, you have robbed the buyer through the operation of a fraudulent edifice. Second, a naked short sale is in effect *counterfeiting* stock. When you sell something in the marketplace, you are representing that you have possession of that thing or will be able to acquire possession before you are supposed to deliver whatever you have sold. A naked short is an intentional false statement of possession and thus represents to the market that there are more shares of that company's stock in the market than actually exist. Since the corporation that issued the stock is the only one with the right to create new shares, a naked short effectively counterfeits the stock certificates in question. Counterfeiting shares of a company's stock tends to depress the price by diluting the value of all real shares with the newly created fake ones.

Of course, eventually the person who shorts a stock naked will want to cover, or buy back, the naked short position. When the short-seller attempts to do so, he must buy shares. Where do those shares come from? The person you sold the naked short to thinks he has actual shares and not fictitious ones! He may, in the interim, have sold those alleged actual shares to someone else. The act of covering a naked short can thus cause a very serious price squeeze, since the person doing the buying is now trying to purchase something that doesn't actually exist.

■　■　■

Now let's look at the common operation of fractional reserve banking. All modern banking systems operate on this model to one degree or another, and run properly, it is safe and bears little or no systemic risk.

But when the model is abused, it creates distortions in the money supply that look an awful lot like an illegal naked short stock sale, but this time against the currency in question.

When a bank makes a loan, it exchanges money for the loan document in which you promise to pay. We'll simplify the economic flow a bit by assuming there is only one bank in the country and everyone uses that bank, and further, that at the start of the economic world this bank has $10,000 of the founder's capital in it. We will also impose a 10 percent reserve requirement on all funds the bank holds; that is, for each dollar deposited, the bank must reserve 10 cents against possible losses.

Note that deposits in a bank are liabilities, not assets, because a depositor can appear at any time to demand the money and the bank is obligated to pay. The cash received in a deposit, along with the loans the banks makes, constitute the bank's assets as they have economic value.

The balance sheet for this fictional bank in our economy the day it opens looks like this:

Liabilities	[Description]	Assets	[Description]
−$10,000.00	Deposit (Founder)	$10,000.00	Cash (Founder)

On the first day, Joe comes into the bank and wants to borrow money to buy a car. We'll assume for the moment that the value of the car he wishes to buy is greater than the amount he wishes to borrow; that is, he intends to make a down payment that is part of the car's price, and that when the price is reduced by the down payment, he will be borrowing less than the fair market value of the vehicle. He wants a $9,000 loan, the most the bank can lend with a 10 percent reserve requirement, and after satisfying the bank owner that the car is worth much more than $9,000, he gets his loan. Now the balance sheet looks like this:

Liabilities	[Description]	Assets	[Description]
−$10,000.00	Deposit (Founder)	$1,000.00	Cash (Founder)
		$9,000.00	Car Loan (Joe)

In the transaction, $9,000 walked out the door in Joe's hand and was replaced by the paper Joe signed, including the title to the car. The bank's ledger is still balanced. Steve the car dealer will shortly come in and deposit the money Joe paid with, as Steve doesn't want to risk being robbed. After Steve has made his deposit, the balance sheet reads:

Liabilities	[Description]	Assets	[Description]
−$10,000.00	Deposit (Founder)	$1,000.00	Cash (Founder)
		$9,000.00	Car Loan (Joe)
−$9,000.00	Deposit (Steve)	$9,000.00	Cash (Steve)

So far everything is good. Note that the liabilities and assets are, as always, balanced. We have left a blank line to show that the loan made to Joe was funded from the founder's deposit.

It appears that the bank is creating money, but it in fact is not, because the $9,000 that was allegedly created is offset exactly by the value of the vehicle pledged against Joe's loan. Now let's run through this exercise two more times, and then we'll show how it all can go wrong and lead to an insolvent bank and the loss of deposited funds.

Liabilities	[Description]	Assets	[Description]
−$10,000.00	Deposit (Founder)	$1,000.00	Cash (Founder)
		$9,000.00	Car Loan (Joe)
−$9,000.00	Deposit (Steve)	$900.00	Cash (Steve)
		$8,100.00	HELOC (Jane)
−$8,100.00	Deposit (Jack)	$810.00	Cash (Jack)
		$7,290.00	Charge (Mike)
−$7,290.00	Deposit (Cruise)	$7,290.00	Cash (Cruise)

Note that the first set of transactions, Jane's home equity line of credit (HELOC), creates a lien against Jane's house. We'll assume that the bank has proved to its satisfaction that the house could be seized and sold without losing any money, should Jane fail to pay. This loan is thus secured and, at least allegedly, is safe.

Mike, however, charged a cruise. He did this without providing any security in that Mike simply promised to pay later in time. The cruise line owner came in and deposited the money Mike paid with. But what happens if Steve and Jack both come into the bank at the same time and demand their combined $17,100?

The bank doesn't have the money. It only has $10,000 in cash: the last deposit from the cruise line, the $1,000 reserve from the original founder, the $900 reserved from Steve's deposit, and the $810 reserved from Jack's deposit. The rest has been lent and is gone.

If the bank lent against assets when it made loans for the car and the HELOC, then those loans could be sold into the marketplace to someone else. Assuming the loans are good, the bank can sell the debt paper it holds, and by doing so, the bank receives the cash required to pay the depositors. But if the bank can't find someone to buy the loans because it lent money against nothing but hot air—that is, an empty promise to pay and not an asset—then the bank goes bankrupt and the depositors lose their money.

When a bank loan is unsecured, it effectively creates a naked short on the *currency* of the nation it operates in. The money that the borrower promised to pay, at that particular instant in time, doesn't exist as value anywhere in the economy that the bank can convert to cash. This is exactly the same as a naked short seller of stock who promises to deliver shares he doesn't have and can't locate to borrow. In addition, since all loans are made with the intent of profit, there is always an interest expense. That interest expense can cause the current value of a debt carried on a bank's books to exceed the value of the alleged pledged asset at some point in the future, even if the loan is originally sound.

In our financial system, we have many banks, and the merchants in question are likely to deposit their funds in a different bank than the one where the loan was originated. This doesn't matter, as the banks are all interconnected. When you write a check against your bank account and give it to someone, the clearing system is how your check is negotiated at the payee's bank and then makes its way back to yours, where your account is debited. When there is an imbalance between the cash deposited in one place and another, the banks borrow from each other and from the Federal Reserve itself and, in doing so, pay a small amount of overnight interest.

Sound banking requires that you never allow the total of all unsecured loans outstanding at any bank to exceed the amount of capital the investors have put into that bank. In our example, the founder of the bank put $10,000 of his own money into the institution as capital. So long as the bank never lends more than $10,000 unsecured at any one time, the worst thing that can happen is that the founder loses his investment. But as soon as the bank is allowed to issue loans on an unsecured basis that exceed the capital that was paid in, retained from earnings, or borrowed from someone, then the depositors are at risk because the bank will not be able to raise the funds necessary to pay the depositors if they show up and demand their money or if the loans that were made later prove to be uncollectable.

Real banking in our financial system has other features that serve to distort this basic set of equations. Hidden in the troubled assets relief program (TARP) bill of 2008[10] was a nasty little provision that effectively removed *all* reserves from the banking system by accelerating a previous law enacted in 2006.[11] Worse, there is a legitimate argument to be made that banks in today's market don't actually reserve anything or fund from actual money, whether deposited or otherwise, despite alleged requirements to do so. Instead, they write loans first, an act that is functionally identical to counterfeiting, and then go looking for the funds necessary to capitalize their actions retroactively, relying on the interbank market for borrowing, if necessary, to make the reserve ratios work. Those distortions just make the banking system more dangerous and add to naked shorting of the currency, rather than assisting with financial stability. The removal of reserve requirements is especially destabilizing as it allows a bank to literally create infinite amounts of leverage and credit with nothing securing the loans that the bank makes.

The basic principles of financial leverage and sound banking are not difficult to understand. Sadly, they are also easily overlooked, and when exceptions are made, the claim usually advanced is that the violation of these rules of safety and soundness are temporary and necessary for some particular social or political purpose. In truth, there is no safe means available to break any of these fundamental mathematical constructs. When basic safety and soundness are ignored, there is inevitably set in motion a series of events that give the rich and powerful the ability to skim funds from the rest of the economy. These distortions then compound, with the wealthy effectively stealing more and more of the economy's output until a breaking point is reached, and a crisis ensues.

Chapter 3

The Aughts or the Aught-Not-Haves

Understanding the fundamental nature of mathematics as it applies to leverage and how banking and other financial institutions can pervert a lending system by effectively counterfeiting the nation's money, we next must turn to how all of these abuses were manifested in the economy during the 2000s.

The technological revolution in the 1980s and 1990s brought computers into the realm of both the consumer and small-business marketplace. While large-scale computers were in American business as early as the 1950s, even in the 1970s and early 1980s, they were unaffordable for smaller enterprises, and analysis of large data sets was impractical. The first Winchester disk drives appeared on the scene in the early 1980s and immediately began shrinking dramatically in both price-per-unit of data stored and size, making mass storage and processing of data practical in other than a mainframe environment. In addition, the processor and memory resources necessary to massage huge data sets became reasonably affordable for corporations of any size.

This in turn led to an orgy of complicated financial instruments that were impossible to construct and understand without the assistance of computerized modeling. This complexity was used as a tool of obfuscation, hiding the basic nature of these financial products from virtually everyone while providing a means of skimming off fees from the ever-increasing transaction volume. With the true risks hidden in these instruments, leverage was piled upon leverage, compounding the economic damage and distortions that lay under the 2007 top in both the real-estate and stock markets and their subsequent collapse.

■ ■ ■

Does anyone remember the famous book by David Lereah, *Why the Real Estate Boom Will Not Bust* (Crown Business)? In it, he opined that real estate was in a perpetual state of price advancement. The book spent its time talking about paradigm shifts in the housing market that would continue to produce outsize price advances, continuing for at least the next 10 years. The book was published in 2006.

This was not the only work that argued for a new prosperity through house price appreciation. Many economists argued that a perpetual 10 percent or greater appreciation in home values was reasonable for the foreseeable future, and most authors cited population and economic growth as part or all of their argument. Even Ben Bernanke of the Federal Reserve chimed in as late as July 2007 that he believed "[housing] sales should ultimately be supported by growth in income and employment."[1]

The problem with these prognostications was quite simple. The top-line growth in GDP, domestic output of all goods and services in the United States, averaged only 6.6 percent from 1953 to today, 4.9 percent from 1990 onward, and 4.2 percent from 2000 forward.[2] In addition, the average population growth in the United States is about 1 percent annually. This made the forward outcome of these prognostications mathematically impossible. Eventually, the price of houses would run away from incomes and thus exceed the ability of people to afford a home. Worse, as will be explained later, the entire premise of alleged GDP growth since the 1980s was predicated on a Ponzi-style scheme of debt accumulation rather than advancing economic output. The only argument to be raised and debated was *when* the collapse in home prices and sales would happen, not whether it would occur.

The damage done by the housing bust was not limited to a small segment of speculators. During the early 2000s, houses were widely touted not as a consumer durable—that is, a place to raise a family and hang your hat—but as investments intended for capital appreciation. Far worse, the use of the inherent leverage in most home transactions was touted as one of the best ways to make money in what was claimed to be a new economy.

Homebuyers don't generally think of themselves as being leveraged, but in point of fact they are. This very fact was exploited by Wall Street and its cadre of financial market participants. Key to the mass delusion of the early 2000s was convincing as many people as possible that their homes were a convenient ATM that would spit out $100 bills on demand. That mass delusion in turn allowed bankers to skim off hundreds of billions of dollars for themselves from a market that was destined to collapse.

When you buy a home with a mortgage, you are inherently engaged in a leveraged financial transaction. Let's assume you put down 20 percent of the purchase price and borrow the rest. Your leverage in the transaction is 5:1. If the home's value declines by 20 percent and you have to sell the house, you will lose all of the money you originally invested. See Figure 3.1.

Note that general consumer price inflation during the years 2000 through 2007 was a compounded 25.1 percent.[3] But home prices, adjusted for inflation, rose much faster, while incomes, adjusted for inflation, did not rise at all. As prices rise, both the amount of money you have to borrow and your monthly payment increases. This leaves you with less disposable income after servicing your mortgage debt each month. In addition, a new buyer has to save even more for a down payment to enter the market. These facts act like a pincer on the buyer in that the prospective purchaser has to save from ever-dwindling free cash flow to fund his down payment, and the size of both the down payment and the monthly payment is rising over time.

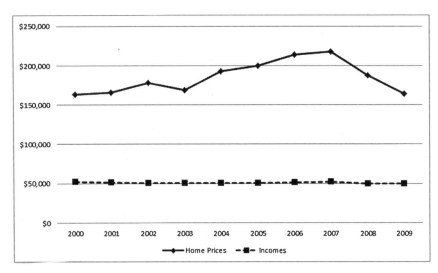

Figure 3.1   Median Home Price and Income with Inflation
SOURCE: Inflation-adjusted income data from the census department, (www.census.gov/hhes/
www/income/data/historical/household/H08_2009.xls), inflation data from the BLS (ftp://
ftp.bls.gov/pub/special.requests/cpi/cpiai.txt), and census median home prices January of each year
2000–2009 (www.census.gov/const/uspricemon.pdf).

This, if left alone, chokes off price increases in excess of income growth in the economy before a bubble can form and do serious economic damage.

This set of facts limited the growth of the housing industry to about 1 percent a year, tracking growth in the population, beyond the actual increase in productive economic output and inflation. The obvious way to be able to sell more houses at higher prices is to reduce the down payment required. With lower down payments, the buyer needs to save less money before making a purchase. But if a buyer puts down 10 percent instead of 20 percent, he is levered not at 5:1 but at 10:1, double the leverage. If the home's value goes down by 10 percent, that buyer has now lost everything he put in. At 3 percent, that same buyer is levered at 33:1, and at the infamous zero down we saw at the height of the bubble, financial leverage is infinite.

The other side of the transaction, of course, is that if a buyer has to put down only 5 percent on the purchase instead of 20 percent, and the price of the home goes up by 5 percent, that buyer has now doubled the money he originally invested. For every yin in leverage, there is a yang, and the increase in potential profits that came from the reduced down payment requirement was instrumental in driving the real-estate bubble. As the bubble engrossed the nation, various real-estate developers and lenders, especially with regard to condominiums, saw great interest from speculators who began to flip property before it had even been constructed. Reports of 100 percent gains on the actual capital invested after a few weeks or months became commonplace.

Of course, this analysis ignores the transaction costs involved in buying and selling a home. The typical real-estate commission is 6 percent and comes out of each transaction. There are also closing costs and fees associated with real-estate transactions, such as documentation stamps on the title to the property, stamps on the mortgage, appraisal fees, and costs for title insurance, plus, of course, the cost of physically moving your household. As such, if you put down less than about 10 percent on a real-estate transaction, you are instantly without equity on the day of the closing. Looked at this way, it is almost impossible to justify down payments of less than 20 percent and simply insane to argue for them under 10 percent, as the buyer with a zero-down mortgage is upside-down on the date the purchaser obtains the keys.

If you're astute, you'll also observe that while such a reduction in down payment changes what you can sell to the consumer, it does nothing to change the outcome predicted by the graphs in Chapter 2. You would expect banks that are full of people who understand these facts to balk rather quickly at the idea of loosening lending standards in response to slackening demand.

Instead of backing off, however, the banks lobbied Congress to relax various laws related to lending and securities transactions, along with seeking ways to stick someone else with the ever-escalating risk.

That move began with Fannie Mae and Freddie Mac. Fannie was constituted as a government support program in 1938 during the Great Depression as part of the New Deal. Its purpose was to provide federal backing to local banks to stabilize the housing mortgage market. For the first 30 years of Fannie's life, it held a near-monopoly over the secondary market for home loans, as it was not only government sponsored but also government owned and operated. In that role, it held only government-backed mortgage paper.

This changed in 1968, when in response to complaints of monopoly activity and pricing, the government split Fannie Mae into two parts, a private corporation still called Fannie Mae and Ginnie Mae, which retained the government-underwritten book of business for FHA and VA-insured housing loans. In 1970, Fannie was permitted to buy and trade privately issued mortgages, and Congress created Freddie Mac, also a private corporation, to provide competition to Fannie.

The two corporations started issuing what we now call mortgage-backed securities (MBS), which gave the public a means to purchase both the cash flow and the success or failure of mortgage debt through the public markets. In theory and the black letter of the law, mortgage bonds issued by these institutions had no actual federal backstop, but we would learn in 2008 that this was not true in practice. The banks, for their part, became the sales conduit for these mortgages, originating them to borrowers and then immediately selling the mortgages off to Fannie and Freddie. It was thought that the control and backing of the federal government would maintain lending standards at a high level, and as a result, there would not be a significant degree of risk in the debt that was passed through and sold by Fannie Mae and Freddie Mac.

The pundits and financial analysts were wrong.

The banks found that they could, using the model of Fannie and Freddie, package private-label mortgages in the 1980s and 1990s and get people to buy those mortgage-backed securities as well. These private-label MBS became quite popular, as they had yields that were significantly higher than Treasury bonds and yet were thought of as generally safe. Twenty years went by with nothing more than a few regional economic problems, such as parts of California in the 1990s linked to military base and manufacturing closings, to disabuse the public, insurance companies, and pension funds from buying these allegedly safe bondlike instruments.

As house prices rapidly rose in the early years of the 2000s, the market reached a saturation point with regard to home buyers, even with relaxed down payments. For decades, there were two gold standard qualifications for a mortgage loan, known as the front-end and back-end ratio. You were considered well qualified for your loan if you spent no more than 28 percent of your gross income on the principal, interest, property taxes, and insurance (PITI) for your home and had no more than 36 percent of your gross income consumed by all debt service combined. Under these ratios, the household that earned a median $50,000 a year income[4] could afford no more than $1,167 per month for PITI. With interest rates running around 6 percent and assuming $200 a month for hazard insurance and property tax, the maximum amount such a buyer could finance on a conventional 30-year fixed loan was about $162,000.

But that home price assumed the applicant had little in the way of other debt. During the early 2000s, Americans were in love with new cars, big-screen TVs, and similar consumer goods, most of which they financed. They also had student loans to pay off, which had become all the rage in the 1990s. The traditional guidelines left just $333 a month for all other debts combined, and that $333 was barely enough for one modest new car payment and the requisite insurance.

The law of immutable financial reality threatened to cut off the housing boom just as it was really getting started, as safe lending prevented further price appreciation. In response, the banking industry did what it always does when its profits are about to get squeezed: They looked for a way to talk people into funding loans that made no economic sense.

First to go was the requirement to have a large down payment. But that didn't get the banks very far because of the basic ratios that had guided mortgage lending for decades and the fact that those consumers without down payments usually lacked them because they were already spending more than they made. If you can't save for a down payment, how will you cover the inevitable leaking roof or bad refrigerator and still pay your mortgage?

Next to be attacked were the ratios themselves. So-called liar loans showed up, where one could state an income but provide no evidence that the income was actually earned. Along with liar loans came no-ratio loans, those in which there were no tests of income and debt payments, and finally a loan called ninja (for *no income, no job, no* *a*ssets). Most of these loans were underwritten by exactly one thing, a high FICO score. But a FICO score only denotes ability to pay your credit card and phone bill on time and says nothing about whether you can service the new debt represented by the house you are trying to purchase.

The banks started packaging these loans into MBS and selling them. Some investors balked for borrowers of modest means and poor credit histories, arguing that they couldn't possibly pay as agreed. The financial industry responded with yet another product, the now-infamous 2/28 and 3/27 subprime mortgages. These loans had a very low interest rate for the initial two or three years and then jumped to 10 percent interest or more. To make these loans more appealing to investors, the mortgage also came with a large prepayment penalty to lock the borrower into at least some period of high interest rates and thus outsize profits. These loans were sold to people who had poor credit and were often minorities with the pitch: "You, too, can buy a house with this mortgage. If you fix your credit up in the first two years, you'll be able to refinance into something more affordable before the rate resets."

Finally, when the ever-increasing price of houses driven by loose lending practices drove pretty much everyone out of the market, the banks and financial industry began pushing what came to be called the option ARM. This was a loan that often had reduced or no docu-mentation required, with yet another twist. The buyer could make one of three payments every month at the borrower's option: a very small payment typically amounting to 1 or 2 percent interest plus a margin and index on the principal value, an interest-only payment at the normal interest rate, or a normal, 30-year amortizing payment. These loans immediately became almost the entire market in parts of the nation known as the Sand States: California, Arizona, Nevada, and Florida. Within one year, 80 percent of all mortgages in these areas were option ARMs, and nearly everyone made only minimum payments.

The ordinary 30-year $500,000 mortgage at 6 percent interest would come with a nearly $3,000 monthly payment. Under traditional ratios with another $1,000 reserved for taxes and insurance, this required an annual income of $185,000. Interest-only, the payment was $2,500. But some option programs permitted a payment under $1,100!

Qualifying a prospect on the option payment allowed someone of modest means, such as a household with under $50,000 in annual income, to buy a $500,000 house and meet the ratios.

Of course, there was a catch.

First, the remainder of the $3,000 you would otherwise pay, or $2,000, got capitalized into the principal balance. That is, the amount of money you owed on the house actually went up each and every month. Worse, at a fixed point in time, the loan would recast to a fully amortized payment for the remainder of the original term. This recast often caused the payment to triple overnight, virtually guaranteeing a default.

The banks knew this would happen when they sold you the loan, and it was disclosed, if you read the fine print. The banks had no reason to believe you would ever be able to pay on the original terms, but they didn't care: They expected you to come back and refinance into a new loan before the recast happened, and they weren't actually holding the mortgage themselves. The bank immediately packaged the loan and sold it to someone else, so if you were unable to pay, the investor and not the bank was on the hook for the bad loan and the loss. Further, with the hook set for what amounted to a forced refinance in a few years if prices continued to appreciate, they would be able to extract yet another bundle of money from you in fees.

This highly complex securitization model was sold to consumers and investors by essentially telling them that they could get something for nothing. Consumers were told they could buy a house for far less than they could rent the same house. Investors were sold on the projected safety of these securities, based on alleged loan characteristics that were unverified and ratings that proved to be worthless. In truth, you can't rent a thing, including a house, for less than the long-run cost of purchasing it because renting that house requires someone else to buy it first and then rent it to you. Since the owner will always seek to make a profit, on balance, renting must always cost more than buying over time.

Getting something for nothing is not possible. It cannot happen in the physical world, and it doesn't happen in the financial world, either. The more complex a deal, the higher the cost, simply because everyone who touches the transaction insists on being paid.

Let us presume that there are two loan products. One is very simple: A person with capital lends you the money to buy a house on some set of terms that fit on two sides of a piece of ordinary paper. The second is extremely complex: You borrow the money from a bank, which then sells the paper to a securitizer, who then transfers it to a depositor, who then signs it over to a trustee, who then issues a bunch of securities of different grades and risk profiles, all of which are allegedly supposed to get some part of your payment and some of the loss if you default. All of this is governed by a several-hundred-page legal document.

Which is the cheaper loan for you, the home buyer? Because nobody works for free, the first one is. This will be true every time, assuming that in both cases the risk you represent is accurately disclosed and priced to everyone involved. It cannot be otherwise in aggregate across the entire body of loans that are made, simply because nobody ever works without being paid in some form or fashion, and everyone involved in commerce seeks a profit.

A competitive market in which there are both simple and complex loans with no misrepresentation by omission or commission will always result in the combination of the lowest cost to the borrower and highest yield to the lender across the entire population of both lenders and borrowers residing in the *simpler* loan. The only way the complex loan can both yield more for the lender and be cheaper for the borrower in aggregate is for someone in the chain between the borrower and the lender to lie in some way so that the lender misprices the risk, or the borrower must overpay. In a free marketplace, one would expect the complex loan to either not be offered or be quite unpopular because the more complex lending structure is uneconomic when compared with the simple one.

When the lending market is analyzed from the top down during these years, it becomes apparent that the entire mortgage marketplace was turned into a fee- and asset-stripping game, designed to transfer consumer and investor money into financial market participants' pockets. The financial geniuses that put these lending systems together were well aware of what was going to happen eventually, even though they couldn't tell you in advance exactly when the catastrophe would occur. By forcing borrowers to come back and refinance before the exotic loan features blew up in their faces, these loans guaranteed future fees and an income stream for the bankers, funded from price appreciation in the house. That price appreciation, in turn, was created by continually loosening credit standards to entice increasingly marginal buyers to enter the market and attempt to purchase homes they could not afford. The consumer obtained little or none of the appreciation in substance, as all of the negative capitalization, unpaid interest, and fees were rolled into a new loan, adding to the amount the consumer would have to pay in the future. Investors, for their part, were led to believe that the risk of their lending was much lower than it really was, and as a result, they underpriced the use of their capital.

The average consumer as a home buyer and the investors who put up the capital bore all the risk. The consumer risked foreclosure or purchasing a home at a grossly inflated price compared with its actual value, and the investors risked ruinous loss when the inevitable day arrived when prices stopped going up and refinancing became impossible. The willful suspension of disbelief in the common law of business balance—that is, the fundamental inability to obtain something for nothing—was goaded on by creating complex financial instruments that were virtually impossible to understand in full, often with hundreds or even thousands of pages of descriptions, legal structures, and disclaimers, before they were purchased. These investments were then sold on a literal "trust me" basis to investors worldwide.

■　■　■

Leverage abuse, of course, was not confined to home mortgages. Everyone believes they deserve a new car, and during the early 2000s, virtually everyone seemed to have a new vehicle every two years. Once again, the usual paradigm for lending started off with a big down payment because a new vehicle depreciates by 20 percent when it's driven off the lot.

After 9/11, there was a huge push to get people to buy new cars. The Bush administration was allegedly involved in the promotional effort in an attempt to prevent a deep recession from coming out of the terrorist attacks that occurred right after the Internet bubble. While zero-interest loans were available during these years on cars, they were strictly limited to good credit risks and the term was held to no more than 36 months.

But the limited term on these loans soon crimped the market for cars; a $40,000 SUV would have a monthly payment of some $1,100. Desperate to drive automobile sales, banks made money easier, with terms extended to as long as 72 months and credit standards declined. Dealers started not only selling cars with zero down payments, they were willing to roll over the existing balance on your previous loan into the new vehicle, sometimes to as much as 125 percent of the new car's value!

This sort of lending was idiotic for both lenders and borrowers. If you executed one of these rollover deals and then wrecked the car on the way home, you could easily find yourself owing nearly half of the price of the now-destroyed vehicle. If you lost your job while still upside-down, with no down payment and 125 percent of the new value of the vehicle financed, you would almost certainly wind up with the car repossessed, as you would be unable to sell the vehicle for more than the remaining balance on the loan. When the economy turned south, there was a flood of repossessions, ruined credit, and even lawsuits by the lenders in an attempt to recover the unpaid balance.

But the damage did not end with car buyers. Presented with false demand as a consequence of these loose lending practices, car manufacturers built and staffed plants to produce vehicles that had no actual economic demand in the marketplace. With the cost of financing effectively negative, vehicle sales shifted from automobiles to light trucks, which were more expensive, had a better profit margin for the manufacturer, and also got poorer fuel economy; trucks went from about a third of all sales to more than half in the space of 15 years. The resulting unsustainable shift in vehicle demand factored materially into the effective bankruptcy of both Chrysler and General Motors and led to the government bailout of both firms in 2008.

"The Heartbeat of America" indeed.

The foolishness of leverage extends to cellular phones, too. Who among us today doesn't have a smart phone? Once they were the tool

of businesspeople; now everyone seems to have them, including children in middle school. On first look, they appear to be cheap. Once
again, the machinations of debt manage to convince you to pull
forward your ability to earn funds tomorrow into a want today.

Most cellular phones are sold under contract. You pay $100 for the
phone and sign a two-year deal for service. You don't think of this as
leverage, but in fact it is. The phone really costs $500, as you will
discover if you ever lose one before the contract is up. Where did the
rest of the phone's price go? The price of the phone was imputed
back into the cost of your monthly service from the cellular carrier,
so the bill that should be $50 a month is $75 plus a mandatory
data plan.

For comparison, you only need to look at services like Virgin
Mobile, which offers a $60 per month unlimited plan for talk, text
messages, and wireless Web. You will have to buy the phone at full
price, but there's no contract.[5]

So exactly how much do you save by choosing to pay for the
phone up front? Sprint offers a similar package as Virgin Mobile for
$80, while Verizon, T-Mobile, and AT&T all want about $100 for their
packages.[6]

In truth, you're paying anywhere from $240 to $480 a year for the
phone, and you committed to a two-year contract. The $100 phone
you picked out in the store, when all is said and done, actually
cost you somewhere between $600 and $1,000! You pay plenty for
the privilege of exercising your leverage in this transaction, and most
consumers never figure out how they've been quite effectively and
legally robbed.

Next, consider a lowly credit card. The new consumer finance law
significantly improved disclosure in that the bank now has to tell you
how long it will take to pay off your bill if you make only minimum
payments, along with how much interest you'll pay in total. Making
minimum payments is a worst-case scenario that is also distressingly
common.

The real scandal with credit cards is what happens if you ever pay
late. Not only will the bank decrease your available credit to zero but
also they will jack up the interest rate to 30 percent and sometimes
more. The banks claim that this pricing change compensates them for

your risk of nonpayment. It can be argued, however, that any person who is a poor enough risk to require these terms to be profitable is someone who will almost inevitably be financially destroyed by this product.

If credit card abuse ended there, it would be bad enough, but it doesn't. There is one bank that is offering a credit card with an unbelievable 79.9 percent interest rate.[7] It also carries a $75 up-front fee and typically has a $300 credit line. The obvious question is whether someone who is a poor-enough risk to apply for such a card will be able to pay the original $75 fee on the first billing cycle and avoid the interest charges, because if you do not and carry a balance, your debt will essentially double every year.

This is not to say that nobody should carry and use a credit card. Credit cards are useful as a tool to avoid carrying cash if you pay off the balance every month. In addition to the convenience, there is considerable safety if a card is lost or stolen, both in the form of federal law and the fact that the thief who uses the stolen card does not have your money but the bank's funds instead. But when credit is used to finance your lifestyle, the cost to you as a consumer is horrifying. As each person spends the credit they have access to, the merchant deposits those created funds back into the bank. The bank is then able to lend out most if not all of those created funds, perpetuating a debt spiral that ultimately is destructive to economic stability. Such an abuse of leverage does severe damage to your standard of living, as every dollar of interest you pay is one dollar you cannot spend on goods and services that enhance your lifestyle.

If you've deduced from all of these transactions that their essence, from the standpoint of the banks and their owners, is to drive transaction volume ever higher and thus skim off a fee without regard to the underlying soundness of the loans being made, you're right.

But the abuses didn't end here; other industries found their own ways to abuse government policies and protection just as the bankers did, spreading the damage even further.

■   ■   ■

Who remembers health care in the 1960s and early 1970s? None of the people beyond the tail end of the boomers do, as they weren't alive yet. But the rest of the public does remember, and we wonder what happened to the days when, running a fever, your parents took you to the local doctor's office and paid $30 or $50 out of pocket with a check to see the doctor. We also remember the annual physical ritual, which our parents wrote a check for an out-of-pocket expense at quite a reasonable cost.

There was health insurance back then, but it was retrospective, not prospective. If you fell down the stairs and broke your leg the hospital would fix you up. Once you were out of the hospital, the insurance company would pay after you submitted the bill to them for reimbursement. There were no preauthorization calls, no surprises, and no $30 aspirins, and few people were bankrupted by medical expenses.

That world, quite arguably a better world when it comes to medical care, is gone.

Today, a huge percentage of the population is uninsured, and we consider that a national disgrace. What's actually a national disgrace is how we have allowed the narrative and discussion on health care to turn the meaning of common words on their ear and turn an aspiration, the desire for good health, into an entitlement.

What we have today is not health insurance. Insurance is something you buy to guard against unlikely events that you could not afford. The practice of buying insurance has to be a losing game for everyone as a whole, since money doesn't magically appear. All actual insurance does is take the total amount of harm that comes to a group of people and spread it out, less a profit for the company aggregating premiums and paying claims.

When you buy fire insurance, it works out well because few people have fires in their homes. When you buy auto insurance, it works reasonably well because the majority of people do not crash their cars in a given year.

But everyone eventually needs health care, and worse, once you need health care on an intensive and continuing basis, such as for heart disease, you then need that care for a very long time. Chronic disease, once contracted, often is a continuing expense for the remainder of your life.

What we have in this country is only partly health insurance. If you suffer an uncommon but expensive event such as a fractured leg, payment for the resulting treatment in a health policy is insurance. But if you look at the common ailments that come with old age, such as arthritis, cancer, and heart disease, they're not uncommon events. Cancer strikes somewhere between one in three and one in two people during their lives; it's a distressingly common disease. Likewise, the flu and childhood vaccinations are not uncommon; the first is a disease that nearly everyone suffers from at one time or another, and the latter are required as you grow from infancy to adulthood.

Our health system in this country is more akin to prepaid health care, with a component of intentionally hiding the cost of our own lifestyle decisions by spreading your lifestyle-driven costs around to others. With an intense fear of mortality, we have created a medical system that feeds on the premise that each person is entitled to the best medical care possible. The bad news is that the companies involved in selling the public that entitlement have every incentive to find a way to renege on the deal they made if the reasonably expected large expenses arrive before the individual involved can be shoved off onto Medicare.

Medicare, the federal health program for older Americans, is one of the worst offenders in regard to distorting the health care market-place. Since the government is such a large buyer of health care in the economy, amounting to more than 20 percent of the entire federal budget, it is able to express its preferences through cost control. Unfortunately, private insurance companies also create distortions in health care delivery, and this, along with antitrust exemptions for insurance companies, means that what a product or service costs in the medical realm depends greatly on how the final consumer pays for care. A private party with no insurance might pay $200,000 for a particular surgical procedure, Medicare will pay only $50,000 for the same operation, and a private insurer may pay $60,000. A routine MRI that costs a person $3,000 on a walk-in basis is billed to Medicare at $500. Disparate billing of this sort, coupled with the effective inability of people to bargain in advance for emergencies and the lack of incentive to do so when insurance covers nonemergency care, is combined with a refusal of the government to enforce antitrust restrictions through legal exemptions. This severely disadvantages anyone who isn't a customer of these preferred programs. The harm from disparate billing is particularly true for those unable to afford insurance at all, as even a routine surgical procedure is very likely to bankrupt the consumer.

If the problems with our medical system ended there, they'd be sufficient to spawn a crisis all on their own. There is, unfortunately, a further compounding issue: a law called the Emergency Medical Treatment and Active Labor Act (EMTALA).[8]

Enacted in 1986, EMTALA provides that hospital emergency rooms cannot turn away someone with an emergent condition irrespective of ability to pay. The legislative record shows that the political motivation to enact this law came from highly publicized incidents of patient dumping during the early 1980s. As with many legislative actions, however, the government's legislative activity did nothing to actually address the issue of cost in these medical procedures, or even the potential liability for missed diagnoses among the indigent. Instead, EMTALA effectively provided the indigent and working poor, including those who are in the country illegally, the ability to bill their medical expenses to every other consumer in the United States at the highest marginal cost by simply showing up in a hospital emergency room anytime they wanted to see a doctor. There is much debate over whether EMTALA was a response to an existing disaster in emergency medical care, particularly among the poor, or whether it created much of the hospital pricing pressures we have seen. But the fact that more than half of all emergency care provided in this country goes uncompensated, and thus is involuntarily cost-shifted to those who can pay, is not in dispute.[9]

Hospitals' and other medical providers' response to these distortions in the market is not unexpected; sheltered from any meaningful competition and exempt from antitrust laws, they engage in behavior that is illegal in other industries. Pricing the same product or service differently for similarly situated customers is normally impossible due to competition and is unlawful in many areas of commerce.[10] Since those with alleged insurance have no incentive to conserve what medical services they consume, medical care suffers from price creep that exceeds inflation by extreme amounts. Some small-group and private plans have seen health insurance premiums more than double over the last couple of years, and price increases of 10 percent or more a year over the decade from 2000 onward are nearly without exception. This is obviously unsustainable since median household incomes have not risen at all in inflation-adjusted terms from 2000 to 2010.

It gets worse. Due to laws enacted as a result of lobbying activity, medical device makers and pharmaceutical companies are able to charge much higher prices in the United States than overseas, with the price difference between a drug in Canada and the United States sometimes as high as 1,000 percent. Normally, this sort of price disparity could not exist; a company that attempted to maintain price control would find people buying their products overseas and then importing the drug back into the United States, forcing domestic prices downward. The drug and device makers have argued that allowing reimportation will result in safety problems and thus have managed to get laws passed banning price competition across national boundaries. Patients in the United States thus effectively pay for the development of nearly every drug and device in the world; the remaining nations then get to use the technological advancement for the much lower cost of reproduction of that drug or device.

How does this all link to leverage? Growth in the cost of medical care greatly exceeds our growth in personal income. We have politically sold an expansion of benefits to the American public, financed by the taxpayer, as help for those who are elderly or less fortunate. We were told that we could broaden the base of those paying for medical care and, by doing so, bring down costs. Unfortunately, economy of scale within insurance works only if the event you're insuring against is rare. This is not true for health care, and yet the consumer only sees the part of their health care and insurance bill that they pay themselves. From the consumer's perspective, health care is often nearly free, while from the perspective of their employer or from the view of society as a whole, health care is a multitrillion-dollar boondoggle. The resulting black hole in the U.S. ability to pay for medical care and the demanded price has been filled with explicit and implicit borrowing by the federal government; Medicare, as just one example, has an estimated forward liability of more than five times our gross domestic product, nearly $80 trillion.

Turning to postsecondary education, we have all heard that success in life is reached through a college degree. This mantra is drummed into us from childhood, and like most of what we're spoon-fed when it comes to matters that have a financial component, the foundation of the claim is largely true. It's the omissions that are troublesome.

Before and into the 1970s and 1980s, it was quite possible to work your way through school with a part-time job at most state colleges. Dormitories were cinderblock-wall affairs with a Formica-topped plank at desk height and a shelf above for your books, along with a pair of beds. There was no air conditioning or cable TV service in the room, and heat was typically provided through central hot water or steam radiators. Food was school cafeteria standard and served in what would be described as a mess hall. Educational buildings were relatively utilitarian affairs, with the money spent in places where it counted, primarily in the labs for the hard sciences.

This is no longer true. Universities have gone on a building spree, constructing housing better thought of as luxury apartments and various emoluments to the educational process that are extraordinarily expensive. Staffing levels have been dramatically increased. Has the quality of education improved? The former environment was sufficient to produce graduates that were behind NASA landing men on the moon, among the many other accomplishments of that time.

But what these increases in spending have done is drive up the cost of postsecondary education to ridiculous levels. And once again, the financial industry and government stepped in to offer a solution to ever-escalating costs via loan programs that can be reasonably described as predatory and abusive.

The first step was, as with housing finance, to petition the government. After all, financial firms wouldn't want young Americans to figure out that they could take out a huge student loan and then default on it! The student's credit would be ruined, and the graduate might have to file bankruptcy, but how could the bank repossess a degree? The answer to that problem was to get Congress to pass a law so that student loan debt was nearly impossible to discharge in bankruptcy. In fact, the only other type of debt that holds the same status in the law as a student loan is child support. Of course, in the case of child support, there's an actual child that requires food, shelter, clothing, and medical care. For student loans, it's just a bank or the government that requires that feeding.

With banks and the government smug in the knowledge that they could hound students forever, cheap, below-market interest rate loans showed up literally everywhere, including direct government-subsidized programs, such as the Stafford student loan. The flood of cheap money caused more people to apply to go to college than there were slots in colleges for incoming freshmen. That shortage of available student capacity led colleges to construct new buildings, renovate dorms, and, of course, raise prices. The basic economics of supply and demand asserted themselves as the creation of artificial demand through cheap-money policies drove tuition and fees higher. This was all to everyone's benefit, since we now had more students going to college, right?

Not quite.

Median family incomes, despite more and more kids going to college, did not rise in inflation-adjusted terms. In fact, the entire 2000–2009 decade was spent with median household income right near $50,000.[11] But colleges were happy to sell you an education that was rising in price at 10, 15, 20 percent or more a year, and it wasn't just tuition and fees that were skyrocketing. Books, housing, food, and everything college related went up in price at outrageous rates. Behind it all were banks and the federal government willing and able to give Junior a ticket to a great education. Whether Junior graduated with tens of thousands or even over $100,000 in debt, and in many cases was unable to find a job upon graduation, didn't matter to them at all.

Part and parcel of this abuse is what is known as the Free Application for Federal Student Aid (FAFSA). This document demands not only information of the would-be student but also of their parents! Without full disclosure of parental income and assets, the student is effectively cut off from *all* grants, scholarships, on-campus work opportunities and federal student loans. Although our youth in college are typically legal adults, if their parents make too much money, there's no aid forthcoming for that student, only debt.

High school and college counselors still claim that college is a good investment. For some people, it is, even at today's ridiculously bloated price, especially if you can qualify for an academic scholarship. But for other students, it is not a good investment at all; graduating with $100,000 in debt when your job pays $50,000 a year and you have to pay off those loans within 10 years is a serious problem. Remember the rule of 72: For most student loans and a 10-year repayment period, it is not uncommon to pay a 30 percent premium for your education once you include the interest charges. If your blended interest rate includes some subsidized Stafford loans and some unsubsidized or private loans, the interest rate charged may be 6 percent or more. On a 10-year amortization schedule, $100,000 in debt costs about $1,100 a month, and on a $50,000 annual salary, you *gross* only $4,167 a month before taxes. Any hope such a graduate had of buying a house and starting a family is gone instantly with this debt load, as the student loans alone consume a quarter of their income. It's quite easy to wind up destitute in this situation, especially if the graduate has trouble finding a job, and many graduates these days do.

Why did this happen in the market? First, if you have more people getting degrees, there will be more competition for the available jobs when you graduate. Basic economics tells us that if there is more supply than demand, the price, in this case the wage offered, goes down. Second, our corporations started importing people like crazy from foreign lands via H-1B visas and offshoring whatever labor they could to parts of the world with lower costs of living, driving labor demand and salaries in this country even lower. As a result, not only did the expense of an education go up but also the available return on that investment decreased dramatically.

In the general sense, student loans are never a good idea. Those who are academically talented should be incentivized to go to school with scholarships and other forms of noncash aid from endowments and private sources of assistance. But for the student who is just average, loan programs, especially where the student intends to study in a field where quick and certain salary advances are not realistic, are financial suicide. Our young people are frequently deceived by counselors, and there's no evidence that the high schools in this nation spend any amount of time on this subject or speak to the cost-benefit analysis that any prospective college student should engage in before attending school. There is no clear disclosure in the various financial aid packages explaining how to work the financial ratios that apply to these loan programs, what happens to you when you graduate with a mountain of student debt, and the likely salary range you will have to pay it back with. There is even less disclosure about the fact that such a debt load will make you instantly ineligible for a standard home mortgage. Finally, some private educational institutions are under investigation over allegedly misleading their students with overly rosy claims of salaries earned and successful college completion statistics.

Arguably the worst problem in this regard is that our youth in high school, as they approach the college decision, are not informed clearly and unambiguously of the traps that await them in the financial aid office. We should not accept their remaining uninformed of the fact that if they go into debt for their college education, that debt is not dischargeable in bankruptcy due to those very lenders and schools demanding special status under the law.

There are exceptions, of course, to the general rule that student debt is a bad idea. Owing $5,000 coming out of college after four years with a job paying $50,000 won't break the bank. The payments on that loan total about $60 a month. But as soon as you start talking about financing more than $20,000 or so for a four-year degree, beware. The required payments are real, and they don't go away; if you default, the lenders sell your loan to a collection agency that will immediately hit you with penalties you can't negotiate away, nor can you file bankruptcy to avoid them.

For many students in high school today, learning a trade makes much more sense than a college education. A trade returns income immediately and typically does not involve taking on any debt at all. It is quite difficult to offshore many trade skills, as they must be performed for the customer at the point where that service is purchased. While trades may not be prestigious vocations, they do pay a decent living wage and, wisely chosen, will always be in demand in some form or fashion. In the 1970s, it was common to have a required shop class in which one learned how to work wood and metal, including welding and the operation of a lathe, as early as junior high. Those students who showed desire and aptitude in these classes were encouraged to pursue their passions, whether in woodworking and fine carpentry, auto repair, or metal fabrication. These classes and facilities have largely disappeared over the last 20 years in favor of pushing every child toward college. There are also many trade skills that have grown out of the technology revolution, such as web design and computer repair, along with the traditional trades such as plumbing. When considering the allegedly better salary prospects that come with a college education, students must include not only the cost of the education itself but also the financing, if necessary, to attend, along with the student's aptitude and love of the field of study. While there are many well-paying professional careers that do in fact require a college education, a student should always keep in mind that a job you hate, even if you make good money doing it, will never be something you look forward to when the sun rises in the morning.

If college makes sense for you or your children, after careful consideration of the options, find a way to achieve that goal without the use of debt and save your financial future.

■ ■ ■

How often do you turn on the TV or pick up a newspaper and read something like this? "Earnings are expected to grow 15 percent annually."

Notice what's missing? There's no end date, nor is there any explanation of what's expected to happen when that end date is reached.

The rule of 72 tells us how long such a growth rate will take to produce a double, and then another one. But this rock we live on called Earth is finite; it has a finite mass, provides a finite amount of land and water, and has finite resources. Therefore, infinite compound growth is simply not possible.

Most investing books tell you that the way you compute a reasonable price for a stock is predicated on its expected forward earnings. The two common metrics are price to earnings and its derivative, price to earnings over growth (PE/G). That's all fine and well for today, but the problem with such an expectation is that one has to put forward a time over which the expectation will be met and then ask "When that period of time ends, what value exists in the company at that point?"

That question is almost never discussed in the media when it comes to stock valuations.

When manias in the stock market get going, you have people buying companies not based on earnings history and a forward expectation but on an even more insane measure, multiples of sales. Of course, you can have record sales and go out of business; all a business has to do is price products and services so low that the firm makes nothing but attempts to make it up on volume! As hundreds of companies proved in the 2000 tech wreck, that's a certain path to bankruptcy, and the more the firm sells under those conditions, the faster it goes bust.

Equity—or stock—is inherently ownership of the company. You, along with the rest of the shareholders, are owners, just as you and your best friend might be owners of a corner ice cream store. One of the ways that you can think about stock valuations and the leverage inherent in what you're buying is to look at how many dollars you have to pay in stock to get one dollar of liquidation value. This is called the corporate leverage index and is a simple computation denoted by equity value dvidided by tangible assets less debt, computed from information published quarterly by the Federal Reserve. There are several versions of this index one can compute, but the most relevant excludes both financial and farming businesses. See Figure 3.2.

This ratio historically hovered between 0.4 and 1.25 from the 1950s until the mid-1990s. When the index dipped under 1.0, you

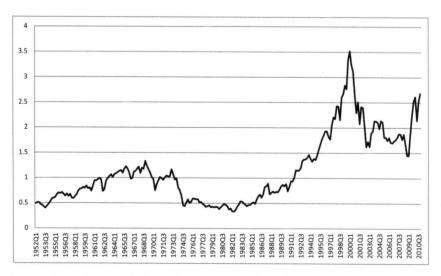

Figure 3.2   Leverage Index, Take 1: Nonfarm/Nonfinancial Corporate Leverage
SOURCE: Federal Reserve Z1 as of March 10, 2011.

were getting a good buy in stocks as you were buying more than a dollar of liquidation value, at least in theory, for each dollar you invested. But as this index rises, you are paying more and more for each dollar of actual tangible value in the enterprise.

This is not to say that when this index is high, it cannot continue higher, or that intangibles such as customer loyalty and innovation do not have value. Witness what happened in the mid-1990s, when valuations first surpassed 1.5. If you looked at this chart at that time, you would have sworn it was a good time to sell everything or perhaps even sell the market short, betting on a decline. Shorting the market at that point would have ruined you over the following several years.

Intangible value, that is, goodwill and intellectual property, is much like the wind. Intangibles have great power when concentrated, and yet they dissipate and indeed often disappear without warning. When intangibles are all a company has inflating its stock price, anything that upsets the market's perception tends to create an instantaneous and ruinous price decline. Without the floor of tangible assets underneath equity value, executives in a firm are reduced to begging investors not to flee or lying about future prospects when sentiment turns sour.

Even after the crash that followed the index reaching a high of 3.5 in early 2000, prices and debt decreased only enough to reduce the index back to about 1.5. Nonetheless, that was more than a 50 percent reduction, with most of the loss coming from stock price declines. A 50 percent loss is, for most people's portfolios, ruinous.

The 1973–1974 recession also saw a significant decline in this ratio, as did the relatively mild recession in 1969–1970.

But notice what happened during the 2007–2009 stock market collapse, shown in Figure 3.2. The leverage ratio didn't move downward much, retreating to just under 1.5, and indeed it shot violently upward in the first quarter of 2009. Right as the market was bottoming, the leverage index began to skyrocket, and corporate leverage continued higher as the so-called recovery took place.

The balance sheet analysis in Figure 3.3 shows you how all of this has happened in the markets. From 1953 to about 1991, stock prices for nonfarm, nonfinancial businesses had never managed to achieve a level materially beyond that of tangible assets owned free

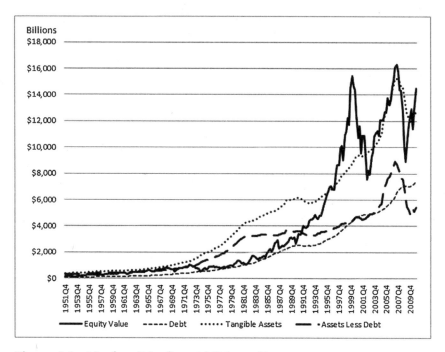

Figure 3.3   Nonfarm/Nonfinancial Balance Sheets
SOURCE: Federal Reserve Z1 as of March 10, 2011.

and clear—that is, above the level of assets less debt taken to carry them. The 1990s stock bubble was a simple mania, a belief that all trees would grow to the sky. When this bubble collapsed and valuations came down, the next attempt was to pretend that tangible assets were rapidly expanding in value, in this case, real estate. That bubble then collapsed, returning the level of assets less debt to that of approximately 10 years ago. At the same time, however, we've witnessed yet another "trees grow to the sky" bubble magically appear in stock prices, entirely unsupported by actual "free and clear" asset valuations.

How is it that corporate valuations moved skyward to above the levels of 2000 in 2007, and how was this bubble that the markets have been enthralled with from 2009 to 2011 generated?

Financial firms were permitted, as a consequence of regulatory capture and the near-extortion of the Financial Accounting Standards Board (FASB) by Congress in the spring of 2009,[12] to hold alleged assets at values that grossly exceeded their price in the market. During that congressional hearing in the spring of 2009 Representative Kanjorski said:

> "If the regulators and standard setters do not act now to improve the standards, then the Congress will have no other option than to act itself. Fair-value, which requires companies to mark assets to reflect market prices, has produced numerous unintended consequences."

In point of fact, FAS 157, the regulation in question, did not require market prices to be used in all cases. What FAS 157 did include was a rule-based means of determining value, as opposed to a financial institution simply deciding to adopt virtually any current value it desired for certain assets rather than forcing them to use market prices. What the banks wanted in that hearing, and got, was the ability to say "trust us" on the worth of the assets they were holding.[13]

This change in standards prevented the deleveraging that otherwise would have occurred and the liquidation of the bad debt that had piled up during the previous 20 years. We see the effects of this change today in the form of mortgage modifications offered to homeowners where the final terms offered include a huge balloon payment, typically after 20 or 25 years. These loans are automatically considered money-good under the new rules, even if the home's value is well below the reworked mortgage amount and will be underwater for a decade or more.

In 2010, we often heard that companies had record cash or even too much cash on the firm's balance sheet. Like so many talismans that are put forward by the media, the record cash claim is a true statement but only half the story. The other half of the story is that companies took on record amounts of debt during the previous two decades, and very little of that debt has come back off from 2007 to 2010. You can see this impact in the preceding figure; there has been effectively no actual liquidation of debt in the corporate sector at all, yet asset valuations have contracted to levels last seen in 2003. Put another way, corporations are holding about 50 percent more debt against those assets now than they were in 2003. At the same time, corporations have shifted more and more production overseas to contract houses and own little or none of the means of producing their products and services. While there are those who argue that intangibles, particularly intellectual property, are just as valid a measure of value as traditional property, plant, and equipment, the fact remains that a host of nations, especially China, bear no allegiance to our claim of intellectual property rights and literally steal anything that's not nailed down.

In the end analysis, the only stable value a business has is the free cash flow the business generates that inures to the benefit of shareholders in the form of dividends. When interest rates are extremely low, the argument is often made that dividend payout ratios on the index as a whole represent a good return. As of spring 2011, the S&P 500 is returning just under 2 percent, the Nasdaq 100 0.6 percent, and the Dow 2.4 percent in dividends. Compared against a certificate of deposit at the local bank, this argument looks valid, and were the leverage index at or below 1.0, the investor would have sizable downside price protection on stock holdings. Unfortunately, with the index standing over 2.5, it is entirely possible to lose 50 percent or more of your money in the stock market from a speculative collapse. When looked at this way, with a risk of loss exceeding 50 percent to earn a 2 percent return plus possible capital appreciation, the argument for owning stocks becomes questionable indeed.

In historical terms, bear markets bottom with the dividend payout ratio exceeding 5 percent and the leverage index well under 1.0. Such a market has little if any speculative premium, and in many cases, equities have actually sold at a *discount* to the liquidation value of the company. Those are the times when a true generational buying opportunity has arisen. No such event has occurred since 1990, despite claims to the contrary by various pundits both in print and on TV.

■ ■ ■

Now let's look at the leverage dynamic from a different angle. Corporations have pushed a 10 percent revenue and earnings growth expectation for more than a decade. We've come to expect rapid growth from the stock market in the general sense. Indeed, investors are told repeatedly that they should expect 10 to 12 percent stock price gains on a long-term basis. Pick up any financial newspaper or book, and that's what you'll find inside. You'll recall that this results in the price of stocks doubling every five to seven years.

For how long can that doubling continue? It can continue for a long time, and it has, but it will not continue indefinitely. As corporations get to the limit of what they can gain in productivity from their domestic workforce, they continue to seek ways to keep the magical 10 percent growth number on the board, quarter after quarter.

The largest single expense for virtually any company is labor. The obvious move for any corporation that finds itself being squeezed between Wall Street expectations and the cost of operations is to find somewhere in the world that has people who are intelligent enough to perform the labor that needs to be done with the lowest possible current standard of living and move operations there. It helps if that same nation also doesn't care much about environmental issues, which represent another cost center, especially for firms that manufacture products using toxic chemicals.

A simple example will make this clear. Let's assume you and your neighbor both run oil-change businesses in your town. You do everything by the book. You hire only U.S. citizens or legal residents, recycle all your used oil and coolant, make sure that the water used to wash down your bays in the evening goes through a separator so any petroleum products are captured, and properly dispose of all the contaminated things that come out of the cars you service in accordance with both good stewardship of the environment and the law. This costs you quite a bit of money and time, not to mention a reasonably high wage paid to your employees, which they enjoy.

Your neighbor, on the other hand, has no such compunctions. He hires all illegal aliens, works them like slaves, and pays them $2 per hour, threatening to call immigration if his employees squawk. Your neighbor surreptitiously runs a pipe from the bottom of his service bay to the storm drain in the street, so his used oil is disposed of at no cost to him. The used and filthy filters and other things that come out of the cars in your neighbor's shop go right into the municipal garbage can behind the store instead of being treated as the hazardous waste they are.

In this scenario, you will soon be bankrupt because your neighbor's oil changes are $2 cheaper than yours, and his shop completes the work faster as well. There is no way for you to possibly compete with your neighbor's shop so long as he can pollute the environment and hire illegal immigrants at below minimum wage.

This is the canard that free trade advocates argue for. China has a near-slave-labor rate of pay compared with the United States. Most of their citizens are coming from or still living in a subsistence-farming model, and as such, the idea of being paid the equivalent of $5 per day sounds like paradise. It might be, compared with tending a rice paddy and having no money at all. The same holds true to a somewhat lesser extent for India, which until recently also was a land primarily composed of subsistence farmers.

In addition, China has a horrifying pollution problem. Industry is pretty much free to pour whatever it wants into the air and water, and it does. The United States once had smokestacks that belched chemicals into the air and pipes that emptied raw toxins and sewage into the water. In the 1960s and 1970s, fish in the Detroit River were considered inedible due to extremely high levels of mercury and other toxins, and the air surrounding River Rouge steel mills and Wyandotte Chemical stank to a degree that made your eyes burn. Pittsburgh was similarly foul, along with most of the industrial Northeast and Midwest.

The United States made the decision that this pollution was unacceptable and cleaned up our air and water at considerable cost. Other nations have not, giving them an unfair competitive advantage. As soon as it is cheaper for a manufacturer to move a factory to China, where they can blow toxic waste into the air and water, hire people at $5 per day to assemble high-tech devices, and then ship them back to the United States, that's exactly what they'll do.

If you think this is limited to China, you're sadly mistaken. Get on the Internet and Google India sometime. Ignore the nice photo essays from touristy places and instead look at the rest of the nation, which is gripped by bone-crushing poverty, pollution, and filth. A huge percentage of the population has no indoor plumbing or even toilet paper. In large parts of the country, feces are found all over the ground, and the people live in straw huts. They bathe in the Ganges while corpses of both animals and humans float by, and dogs tear at the flesh of the washed-up dead. This is our trading partner, where U.S. businesses outsource call centers today. Of course, those taking the calls in

India require much less in salary than they would, were they U.S. citizens residing here.

Our offshoring of jobs has left an employment vacuum in the nation that used to be the industrial powerhouse of the world. The United States is no longer competitive in manufacturing, not because our people are dumber or our educational system is less effective. We fail as a competitor because we cannot compete with labor that is one-fifth as expensive as a U.S. worker and our foreign counterparts pay nothing for environmental compliance while we capture manufacturing toxins and dispose of them properly. What we're left with in the United States are jobs that cannot be outsourced because the labor's product is either too fragile to survive the time and distance of transportation or the service provided is one that requires hands-on contact, such as medicine and construction.

There are those who argue that this problem is self-correcting, in that as nations like China and India mature, their economies will demand cleaner air and water. This, it is argued, will cause China, India, and other nations to undergo the transformation that we had in the United States with regard to environmental standards and labor laws.

Let's extend today's situation out and assume that premise is not true.

In that case, we wind up with only two groups of employees in this country. There are those who flip burgers or pull coffees for minimum wage, and those who perform services such as health care and construction, where hands-on contact is necessary. Everything else migrates to the part of the world where you can pay someone $5 a day. Then, the people who make $5 a day begin to eat more food than they did before, and those people start to acquire the first bits of aspiration for their future. This in turn presses upward on essential commodity prices such as food and oil, which reflects worldwide into the price of those commodities. The new middle class in these nations find themselves not much better off than they were before industrialization, mostly due to the rising cost of necessities in their life.

Worse, commodity price increases, along with evisceration of our employment base, mean that the standard of living for the majority of Americans falls precipitously. This has already begun. Median incomes in inflation-adjusted terms have not improved over the last decade, yet the real cost of living has gone up substantially. The longer these distortions continue, the more poverty we will see here in the United States. The handful of people who work at the very top in the executive suites and financial institutions make lots of money, but everyone else below them literally starves. Say hello to the Dow at 20,000, while half the United States lives in refrigerator boxes under the nearest freeway overpass. Is this an acceptable future for our nation?

Let's assume instead that nations such as China and India have the sort of sea change toward environmental stewardship and labor that we had in the United States. Wages in those nations rapidly rise, and environmental concerns force the cessation of rampant pollution. The rising cost of production relaxes the pressure on our manufacturing, in that the United States becomes more competitive as China's and India's standard of living improves. But now the entire premise that has driven operating margins for U.S. businesses collapses. The debt load that these companies carry cannot be serviced without the cheap labor they now enjoy. In this case, our stock market collapses, and there are many corporate bankruptcies. Such a reversion to the mean in corporate leverage could easily return the leverage index back to 1, implying a crash in stock market prices of more than 60 percent!

Is there a middle ground? Yes. Our corporations might try to continue to exploit both land and people. As India and China become less competitive, labor will move to places like Somalia. But that doesn't change the end point of the evolution; it merely delays it. The longer we continue to believe that we can export all of our labor to where working conditions are terrible and environmental concerns are nonexistent, the worse the eventual correction to a sustainable economy within our nation will be.

■ ■ ■

Turning next to intentionally complex financial instruments and their abuse, we find derivatives that were at the core of much of the global market meltdown in 2008. Few people outside of active investors understand exactly what derivatives are, or why their abuse is so dangerous and leads to systemic risk.

A derivative is just a financial instrument that is, as the name implies, derived from something tangible. Instead of buying an actual barrel of oil, you can buy a derivative, such as a futures contract, if you wish to speculate on oil prices or lock in today's price, either as a user of oil or as a producer. Active investors are probably familiar with puts and calls, two commonly traded forms of derivatives on stocks. A *put* gives the buyer the right to forcibly sell stock upon someone else at an agreed price; a *call* gives the buyer the right to forcibly buy stock from someone else at an agreed price. These are rights but not responsibilities, and the person who purchases the derivative is the one who is entitled to choose whether to exercise that option. Derivatives have an expiration date, by which time the holder has to either exercise the right or lose it. If the agreed price, called the *strike price*, is in the money at expiration, the derivative is valuable, and if not, it's worthless.

Puts can be seen as a form of insurance. If you own IBM stock, you might be concerned that the price of the stock could drop dramatically at some point in the next year. You can buy a put on IBM to protect against this.[14] In buying a put, you pay a premium for the put to the seller representing the value of time, the anticipated volatility or change in the stock's price, and how far out of the money the contract is, that is, how much of the potential loss you're willing to shoulder yourself.

For every buyer of stock on an exchange, there is a seller. But a person who sells you stock whose price later goes up or down loses only the opportunity to make or lose money. With derivatives, it's different: For every winner in a derivative trade, there is always a loser of an equal amount of money, less commissions and fees.

That is, when you buy a put for $10, someone sells you that put and collects the $10, less the fees on the transaction. But if the stock falls in price to $20 below the strike price, and you exercise your option, while you're protected from the $20 loss, the person on the other side of the transaction loses an actual $20, less what was already collected from you. In this case, you have a $10 profit in the trade because you were protected from a $20 loss, and for that protection, you paid a $10 fee. The seller of the protection is out $10 because he must pay the $20 you were protected from losing, but he collected your $10 premium up front.

The primary legitimate use for derivatives is to protect an investment or required commodity in a business from price changes that could otherwise be severely damaging. An airline might buy a derivative to protect against increases in fuel cost. The airline willingly and intentionally accepts a small cost above today's fuel price to guard against a potential large increase that could bankrupt it. If there is no large increase in price, then the airline is out the money spent for the protection, and the person who sold it to the airline keeps it, just as an insurance company keeps your premium if your home does not burn down. If there is a large increase in price, then the seller of the protection effectively covers the cost of the fuel increase for the airline.

So what's the problem with derivatives?

If derivatives are used the way they're intended, or even used as a tool to speculate on price changes, there's no particular problem. But like most things during the bubble years, derivatives were perverted and abused, and ultimately they presented a false view of financial health among many firms, including banks and other financial concerns.

One type of derivative is a credit default swap (CDS). A credit default swap is a contract that protects against the default of a bond issued by some institution. It can be written against any sort of debt, such as a corporate bond or mortgage security. If you own debt issued by IBM and are concerned that IBM might not pay, you can buy a CDS against that risk. The seller of protection collects a premium from you. If there is no default, he keeps the premium you paid him. If there is a default, then you give to him the bond that you bought the protection for, and he is obligated to give you the face value of that bond. You are thus protected, exactly as you would be if you bought fire insurance on your house and the house then burned down. The seller of the protection, who now has the bond, can then try to collect whatever is available to him on the now-defaulted instrument.

The problem with CDSs is that they're typically sold over the counter. That is, there is no central exchange for these products. If you're interested in buying one, you must call up all of the major financial institutions, such as Goldman Sachs and Morgan Stanley, and ask each individually for a quote. The lack of price transparency is to the big banks' advantage, since you can't get an electronic quote, where everyone is required to bid and offer in the open. The banks can and do exploit this lack of open information to get a better spread, that is, the difference between what someone will sell the protection for and what someone buys it at.

Without centralized exchange listings, there's also no guarantee that the person who sells you this protection can actually pay if the insured-against event actually happens. The bank you buy the contract from normally tries to find someone who will sell the same protection you just bought at a cheaper price. This game of musical chairs frequently goes through multiple iterations as a means of pocketing a bit of money from each step in the transaction.

In the regulated options market, if you sell an option, you're required to be able to clear the transaction that might arise if you are assigned, that is, if you are called upon to perform your obligation. The brokerages that take and fill orders on those exchanges are required by the exchange to make sure you are able to clear those transactions on a nightly basis, because the exchange itself is responsible for making sure your contract is good. If you sell a $100 IBM put, for example, you have agreed that you will buy 100 shares of IBM at $100 each and take them from the buyer if the purchaser of that put wants you to at any time up to expiration. The exact amount of money you must have to sell that put varies, but in all cases, the broker is responsible for ensuring that you can perform your obligation for as long as your contract remains open.

There are also derivatives traded on exchanges for broad stock indexes, such as the S&P 500, and commodities, such as oil, gold, corn, and wheat. In each case, you can buy or sell an option or futures contract that controls a large amount of the underlying commodity or index and then profit or lose from the underlying commodity or index's price movement. Again, your position is margined nightly, and with futures, you must have available in cash any in-the-money amount on a nightly basis if your position goes against you. This margin amount provides a cushion against the possibility of a rapid price change that leaves you unable to perform your obligation, and if that margin cushion is exhausted, your brokerage may forcibly close your position without your consent.

When traded on an exchange, derivative contracts are blinded, and you do not know or care who is on the other side of your trade. The exchange guarantees the contract's performance and randomly assigns the seller to perform if the holder of the right to exercise chooses to do so. Because the exchange collects only a small fee per contract but is responsible for guaranteeing each trade that is worth hundreds or even thousands of times the fee it collects, the exchange has a tremendous incentive to make sure that all brokers that deal with the exchange insure that their customers can perform their obligations. For these reasons, there is no chained counterparty risk as there is with over-the-counter derivatives, and there has never been a default where those who held listed contracts did not get paid, even during the stock market crash of 1987.

This is not true in the over-the-counter derivatives market.

Let's say, for example, you hold a mortgage-backed security that was questionable when it was originally constructed. It contained many loans for which the buyers lied about their income or the bank that originated the loan didn't verify anything. To protect yourself against the people who took out those mortgages not being able to pay, you buy a CDS against the security from some financial institution. Owning that protection allows you to claim on your corporate balance sheet the full value of the security, even as it becomes more and more likely that the security will default and there will be a large loss.

The problem with your claim of protection is that there's no guarantee that the person you bought that contract from can pay you, and the seller is specifically and singularly responsible to you. He may have in turn bought a similar CDS from someone else, and so on. This chain of protection is good only as long as the last person in the chain can pay up. If that last person doesn't have any money when the default occurs, then that default ripples back up the chain, exposing the next person to a loss that he thought he was protected against. While over-the-counter derivatives markets allow someone to *novate*—that is, take over a responsibility from someone else—there's no requirement that a buyer accept the change in responsibility. That is, if you buy an OTC derivative from Goldman Sachs, you may specify and demand that only Goldman Sachs is the party responsible for paying you in the event the triggering conditions are met.

When you heard about the risk of meltdown in the derivatives marketplace during 2008, this is what regulators and pundits were referring to. AIG had an unregulated subsidiary called AIGFP that had written roughly $500 billion in protection contracts, approximately $80 billion on subprime mortgages alone, but had essentially no money in reserve. When the insured event happened, and the mortgages started to go bad, AIG was called upon to pay but was unable to do so. This raised the possibility of a cascade of defaults and bankruptcies that could have collapsed the entire banking system.

But was that possibility of collapse true? Or was it an empty threat?

We'll never know the truth with certainty. But there are two facts to keep in mind. First, most derivative contracts require you to hand over the defaulted instrument to get paid. Second, there were many more derivative contracts sold than there were physical securities in many of these cases. This means that some of the contracts may have been unenforceable since there was no defaulted instrument you could acquire and tender in order to collect. Simply put, the people who entered into some of those contracts did so simply to speculate and never owned the actual underlying security in question, and due to the way the contract was written, they might not have been able to collect anyway. Nonetheless, the claim was made and accepted by the politicians that it was necessary to bail out these firms, including the banks, or economic Armageddon would immediately ensue.

The ripple effect that was believed to be on our doorstep, whether in fact or simply as a threat, occurred as a consequence of the unsound practice of trading derivatives over the counter with no effective supervision. Given the now-evident danger with derivatives traded over the counter, why has the banking industry resisted a change in how they do business in these contracts?

In a word, profits.

When you trade a security on an exchange, there are no real secrets. Everyone's offer to sell and bid to buy must be exposed and is visible to everyone. You also don't know whom you're buying from or selling to. The computer or floor broker obscures that information, making the identity of the counterparty invisible to both participants. All you know is that someone is willing to sell you 100 of X for $Y. Price discovery happens in a clean and transparent manner, because everyone is, at least theoretically, on a level playing field.

With over-the-counter derivatives, there is no central listing at all. The contract you decide to buy from Bank #1 may or may not be at a fair market price. The less information you have in that transaction, the more likely the bank is to be able to effectively rob you. In addition, you are taking on a specific transaction risk with a specific company, and there is no independent third party that is watching out for both parties' interests and guaranteeing that the contract can be performed. Finally, banks and other sellers of protection inherently chain their exposure, which means that the party that thought it was relying on the ability of a given firm to pay believes that the seller of the contact has the actual risk, when that may not be true.

■   ■   ■

This is all rather complicated for the average person on the street to understand; an example that is closer to your daily life is in order. Most of us buy auto insurance. State laws typically require us to have liability insurance in the event we have an accident and hurt someone. The price for that insurance is determined by where you live and your driving record, in that a person who has never had an accident but has driven for 20 years is less likely to crash next year than a person who has a long record of at-fault accidents.

Now let's presume that some new company comes into the market. They sell only auto insurance. For a very attractive price, you can get an insurance card that allows you to renew your license plates and states that you have the legal minimum insurance requirements.

That company then goes out to find other companies, including hedge funds, to write what amounts to an insurance policy on your liability risk. It gets permission from the government, however, to treat this series of transactions as something other than insurance, so nobody can police whether the people trading in that security can actually pay. Through this series of transactions, some of which are not visible to the new company, the firm is able to chain your risk off through multiple other companies, including some of the largest banks in the world.

Let's assume that due to extraordinarily good weather and just plain luck, very few accidents happen for a couple of years. This new insurance scheme looks great for everyone, as you have cheaper auto insurance and the company that sold it to you is making a lot of money and giving huge bonuses to its employees. Its stock price soars.

Unfortunately, the hedge funds they bought their pass-through protection from have no money at all, as they paid it all out in bonuses. The next year the weather is terrible, and all the accidents that hadn't happened over the previous two years occur. Suddenly, this new insurance company has to pay claims but has no money to do so, and the hedge funds and banks that it bought the alleged protection from have no money to pay with either. All of these companies are immediately threatened with collapse.

This is very much like what happened with credit-default swaps. There's no way for the buyer to know if he really does have an actual enforceable claim. Certainly, the buyer has a contract he can allegedly enforce, but if the seller of the protection has no money when the time comes to perform, what he really bought is a worthless piece of paper.

The banks love a market like this. You as a customer get to transact where there's no auction system, and as a buyer you have no way to know whether you are getting a good price or a bad one. You can use the market to claim something you own and is high risk has low risk, and nobody can prove you're lying because you bought protection that gives you alleged insurance against the bad outcome. The person you bought it from never has to prove he has the money to pay you, right up until you try to collect, because the sellers lobbied Congress to make the contracts they're selling immune from regulation. The sellers who have no money love this system because during good economic times, it's a license to steal; they collect a premium so someone else can claim to have no risk in an asset that is in fact very dangerous. When the economy turns down and the bad outcome happens, the seller simply declares bankruptcy and walks away or goes to the government and demands a bailout lest the entire financial system collapse. In the meantime, the seller can bonus out all the money he takes in to their executives and employees. What's not to like about a scheme like this?

Since the Commodity Futures Modernization Act of 2000 (CMFA) was passed in 2000, this is exactly how the banks and other financial institutions have run over-the-counter derivatives. And despite the claims of politicians, the recent Dodd-Frank financial reform bill does not put a stop to this practice, nor does it hold any of the executives or institutions to account for their former sale of alleged protection when they had no money to actually perform on their obligations.

■   ■   ■

The federal government and Federal Reserve employ thousands of mathematicians and statisticians to analyze every aspect of our economy. From the Bureau of Labor Statistics to the Commerce Department to the Bureau of Economic Analysis and beyond, analysis, data tables, and charts are produced on a weekly, monthly, and quarterly basis to allegedly communicate to the public exactly what is going on in the economy.

The Federal Reserve, for its part, produces dozens of analytical publications. The largest and most complete is known as the Z1, formally the Flow of Funds report, which comes out four times a year.

All of these government and quasi-government agencies know everything that has been discussed thus far. Their professional economists and analysts certainly understand the principles of mathematics that govern what's economically possible. It is thus here, from where we are supposed to get unbiased and honest reporting, that the most stinging indictment against economic policy must be leveled.

One can excuse individuals in society who don't understand mathematics and how it relates to the economic world. There's certainly no focus in our educational system on how the magic of compounding is both a blessing and a curse, and yet both are part and parcel of every economic decision and its outcome. That the public is unaware of these facts is unfortunate but understandable.

A willful false statement, otherwise known as lying, is a different matter. In these acts of intentional deception, many major government and quasi-government organs are complicit.

The Great Depression is often claimed to have happened because, in the words of many pundits, "The government and the Fed didn't do enough." That's a blatant falsehood. In point of fact, there was a depression in history just 10 years earlier that is not often discussed. That would be the extremely sharp deflationary recession in 1920–1921.

Many economists and pundits also opine that deflation is catastrophic and must be avoided. In fact, Bernanke himself has made clear that he fears deflation, as did Alan Greenspan.

But 1920–1921 makes clear that this fear is irrational at best.

The 1920–1921 deflation occurred as part of the adjustment following World War I. A large influx of labor occurred as soldiers returned home, and production was realigned to peacetime purposes. The armed forces reduced their employment from 2.9 million to 380,000 by 1920. The economy first underwent a minor recession following Armistice Day as the realignment began, and then a major economic growth spurt took place, with civilian employment and industrial production surging. But those who believed that the postwar period would be one of unbridled economic progress were to be proved too exuberant.

In 1920–1921, prices fell by an astounding 15 percent,[15] a net price change that on a time-adjusted basis was much sharper than in the Great Depression. The fall in wholesale prices was even larger, nearly 37 percent, the most severe for any comparable period in U.S. history. Industrial production fell by nearly a third, automobile production dropped by 60 percent, and unemployment doubled. The stock market was cut in half.

In 1921, Herbert Hoover was commerce secretary of the United States under President Harding. He urged the government to bail out insolvent institutions and prop up the economy, arguing that it would be catastrophic to allow prices to fall while both firms and banks that had taken on an unreasonable amount of leverage and risk were allowed to fail. This advice is stunningly similar to that offered both during the Great Depression of the 1930s and today.

But President Harding refused this advice, instead choosing to allow the market to clear on its own.

The market did in fact clear. While the downturn was extraordinarily severe, the process of creative destruction cleared away bad debt and bankrupt entities. Where there was a manufacturing concern that went bankrupt due to excessive leverage, there was now a vacuum into which new entrepreneurs could sell goods and services. With the economy having been rapidly cleaned of both excess production capacity and debt, and the adjustment in labor and product prices complete, economic recovery was immediate and strong. Within 18 months, full employment was restored, and industrial production rose an astounding 60 percent.

The deflationary depression of 1920–1921 was over, almost before it began.

Contrast this with the 1930s. The advice given to President Hoover was to let the market adjust on its own. But remember, this was the man who 10 years earlier had counseled intervention. He instead intervened in the economy in every conceivable way, and when his intervention failed, President Roosevelt (FDR) interfered even more, along with the Fed. That government intervention by any measure you care to use failed spectacularly and repeatedly. Among government acts undertaken were intentional currency devaluation, bailing out the housing market with the formation of what would become Fannie Mae, price controls, and even the intentional destruction of crops and livestock in a futile attempt to drive farm commodity prices higher. All of this intervention failed to restore the economy to health over a period of more than 10 years. It is, in fact, a fair assessment to conclude that the actions by both FDR and Hoover to prevent the economy from shedding its excessive debt and leverage dramatically extended the Great Depression and caused far more economic suffering than would have occurred if the market had been left alone.

The overall financial leverage picture of the past 60 years is easily understood from Figure 3.4.

The expansion of leverage as a means of boosting apparent economic growth dates to the 1980s. The decisions that have led to the economic state we find ourselves in are both intentional and pervasive; by expanding leverage in the economy, we create the appearance of wealth and growth, but not actual wealth and growth.

Borrowing to purchase something today is nothing other than pulling forward tomorrow's demand. We've all seen the Popeye cartoon

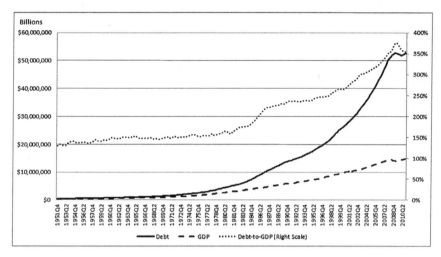

Figure 3.4   Absolute Debt to GDP
SOURCE: Federal Reserve Z1, BEA GDP Table 1.1.5, both as of March 10, 2011.

where Wimpy says, "I'll gladly pay you Tuesday for a hamburger today!" All borrowing to consume is effectively the same scheme that Wimpy repeatedly ran in those cartoons. The demand for whatever goods or services you consume today by taking on debt will not be consumed tomorrow, but you will have to earn the funds to cover the debt plus the interest due. The use of debt is thus justified only to bridge a short-term gap in funding that you are certain will be more than made up for tomorrow—and never for a recurring expense that you cannot pay for in perpetuity out of your income.

Let's assume for a moment that you earn $50,000 a year in your job. You've spent the last 10 years making about that much money, with no real raises of substance. But like many Americans you've been extracting equity from your house and using it to spend about 4 percent more than you make. Each and every year, you have effectively lived beyond your means by turning phantom appreciation in your home's value into purchasing power through serial refinances or the use of a home equity line of credit. You have a smart phone with a $100 monthly bill, a new car every two years on lease, a $120 cable television and Internet package, and two expensive vacations a year.

Then 2008 comes along, and the stock market collapses, the banks come close to failure, unemployment spikes, home prices decline, and consumer sentiment goes in the trash can.

Your boss comes into your office and tells you that the company has to spend more and more on items that do not contribute to production, sales have fallen off, and he can no longer afford to pay you $50,000. He offers you two choices: Be laid off or accept a 40 percent reduction in pay, reducing your salary to $30,000 a year.

You think about this proposal for a while and decide that a job is better than no job, recognizing that you don't really have other options for employment in the current economy. Begrudgingly, you accept your boss's offer of a lower salary.

When you get home, you're in somewhat of a panic. All the debt you've taken on has become an immediate problem. Not only is your home's value below the outstanding mortgage amount and you can't borrow anything more against it, but you've got a monthly cash requirement that is a full 40 percent over the amount of money you take in from your job!

You decide that you're going to say nothing about your horrifying state of affairs. In fact, you're going to lie. You decide that you will tell everyone you're fine and studiously avoid mentioning the salary cut you just suffered. Instead you use your credit cards, which the banks had foolishly granted six-figure credit lines on a couple of years previously, to maintain your standard of living and spending.

This path of action will eventually ruin you. The charade you are running on everyone you come in contact with survives only until the bank figures out that you're never going to pay them. This might happen when you can't make the minimum payments, or it might happen when someone tells the bank that your salary has declined by 40 percent and there is no realistic prospect for you to recover your former rate of pay.

Iceland and Greece both attempted something similar to this on a national level, with Ireland not far behind. In Iceland's case, they decided to pull the plug. That is, they defaulted on some obligations they didn't have the ability to pay, devalued debt denominated in their currency and effectively forced creditors to take a discount on the amount owed, much like a credit card company will settle for far less than the full balance if you really can't pay off the card. While the story is not fully written on the success of Iceland's measures, their economy appears to have stabilized. In Greece and Ireland's case, the solution thus far has been to seek yet more subsidized debt rather than face reality. Their strategy will fail. It mathematically must, unless somehow those nations can run not a deficit but an actual primary surplus, so they can pay both the interest due and some measure of principal.

What other nation has gone into debt wildly beyond its means? We have, right here in the United States. See Figure 3.5.

The solid line is the actual amount of growth in the economy adjusted for government borrowing. Borrowing money doesn't indicate actual growth; it is spending today that you promise to earn tomorrow. As such, every dollar borrowed by the government and spent has to come off the value of actual goods and services created by economic activity, as that borrowing constitutes artificial demand that, but for the borrowing, would not exist.

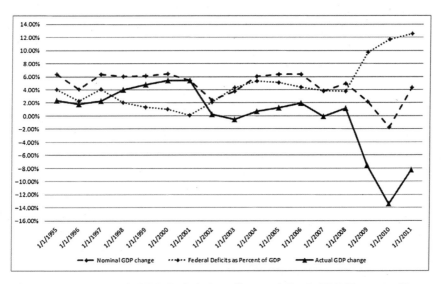

Figure 3.5 Nominal GDP, Deficit Spending, and Real GDP Year-over-Year
SOURCE: Treasury "Debt to the Penny" and BEA GDP Series as of January 2011.

Notice the dotted line. This is the federal government deficit, expressed as a percentage of GDP. The deficit in actual numerical debt accumulation has gone to zero exactly once in the last 15 years, the last year of President Clinton's second term. Contrary to President Clinton's claim, he never ran an actual budget surplus; instead, he used the Social Security and Medicare tax revenues to claim he had one that did not exist.

Unfortunately, 2000 was also the last year we had a strong positive rate of change in domestic output when one adjusts for government borrow and spend.

But would reducing the deficit to zero have provided economic stability? No, because the government is not the only entity that was increasing its borrowing.

To present a true picture of the economy, we must adjust for all borrowing, not just government borrowing. One can take the change in GDP on an annualized basis and subtract from it the total systemic change in debt on an annualized basis. That is, GDP now divided by GDP 12 months ago is the common measurement of growth. But this presumes that one is actually producing the funds to purchase that economic output. That is, commonly reported GDP numbers presume that wages and output by corporations and people are rising and that increased personal income is how we are funding our economic expansion. As has been pointed out, you can, for some period of time, borrow to spend beyond your means. But the goods and services you consume by doing so aren't earned from your output; they're bought with a promise to pay by producing something in the economy tomorrow instead of with either current production or savings.

To properly look at GDP in terms of actual economic progress, one must back out all the borrowing that takes place during the same period, irrespective of who's doing the borrowing. That is, you can argue that the proper method of looking at GDP is to subtract that which is paid for not with today's output, but with promises to pledge tomorrow's production. See Figure 3.6. Looking at it this way, one gets a very different view of alleged growth in the economy, and the depth of the hole we have dug for ourselves becomes clear.

The heavily dashed line shows the gross imbalance in our economic system, or what GDP growth would be reported as, were

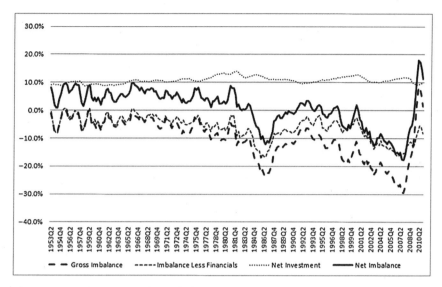

Figure 3.6 GDP-to-Debt Imbalance (Annualized)
SOURCE: Fed Z1 and BEA GDP Series as of March 10, 2011.

we to subtract all newly acquired debt. The top lightly dotted line represents the percentage of gross investment in the economy from government GDP reports, showing that we consistently reinvest about 10 percent of our domestic output back into the means of production, such as factories and mines. And finally, the solid black line shows what level of imbalance we have sustained in the economy since 1953, removing debt taken for investment in the means of production.

Stated this way, our economy stopped growing in real terms in 1983. When adjusted for new debt taken for consumption or speculation, we had an average real GDP growth rate from 1953 to 1983 of 5.29 percent. But in the nearly three decades since through 2009, our adjusted GDP growth rate on an annualized basis was a stunning negative 4.89 percent.

In the early 1980s, we successfully used new debt taken for consumption and speculation to try to pull us out of the deep recession that was triggered by the oil shocks. This action was reasonably successful, in that we were able to get back to a balanced economic picture in terms of debt and GDP by 1991. Unfortunately we were never able to clear that debt and instead leveraged up ever more borrowing to pretend that we had achieved permanent prosperity in our economy. This falsehood was to become painfully apparent in April 2000, when the Nasdaq market began to come apart and then, over the next two years, collapsed.

Beginning in 2001, our nation embarked on a ruinous path of using new debt rather than production to finance yet another false recovery from our leveraged follies. At its peak in the third quarter of 2007, an astounding 17 percent, or approximately one dollar in six, of GDP was being produced by new borrowing for the purpose of consumption.

The spike upward in debt-adjusted growth that began in the fourth quarter of 2009 and peaked in the first quarter of 2010 was due to total systemic debt reduction. This is the very thing the government is trying to prevent, but reducing systemic debt is necessary to bring the economy back into balance.

Looked at another way—on a quarterly basis, as shown in Figure 3.7—we can see how bad the distortion in our economy got and

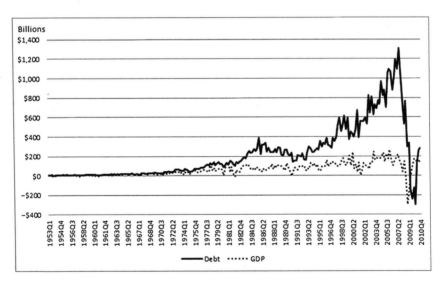

Figure 3.7 Debt and GDP Change, Net-Net Quarterly
SOURCE: Fed Z1 and BEA GDP Series as of March 11, 2011.

for how long we were attempting to cheat mathematics via debt accumulation.

■ ■ ■

At its peak in the third quarter of 2007, while we were being told that the economic damage from subprime mortgages was contained, actors in our economy borrowed $1.3 trillion new dollars while the economy itself generated a mere $150 billion in economic expansion.

The problems we face in our economy today did not occur in a year, two, or five. They are not the fault of either Republicans or Democrats; rather, they belong equally to both major political parties. They have been building as economic imbalances for three decades, dating back to the 1980s. Financing alleged economic growth through increased borrowing is sustainable only if the borrowing increase goes into productive investment—the purchase of assets that are designed to produce a positive economic rate of return. When debt is taken on to finance consumption, you begin walking down the path to ruin, as you are simply pulling forward tomorrow's demand for a car, house, cell phone, or other goods and services into today, leaving you with both the inability to purchase it tomorrow and the interest expense on the capital you have borrowed.

These imbalances are why inflation-adjusted median incomes haven't moved upward at all in the last decade and why it seems to be harder and harder every year to maintain a middle-class lifestyle. These GDP and borrowing numbers are also not adjusted for inflation, which has relentlessly destroyed purchasing power. The loss of purchasing power in real terms, the drive to two-income households, the wild screams from the media, government, and Bernanke's recent assertion that QE2 has been a success because the stock market has gone up[16] all belie the truth: We have not grown the economy at all during the past *30 years* to any material degree. Instead, we have serially pulled out the credit card and said, "Charge it!"

When did stock prices begin to accelerate? In 1991, the S&P 500 printed 300 and the Dow stood at 2,500. That was the beginning of the latest monster bull run in equity prices. But let's not forget the

1980s, which had a similarly foolish dalliance with debt addition, and in response the Dow went from roughly 800 to 2,600. Our latest bull run is a piker compared with that performance. On a percentage basis, we're getting less and less bang from more and more debt.

The problem for equity investors is that *none* of the stock market appreciation has come from actual economic growth. It has all come from ever-increasing amounts of debt leverage that, when subtracted back out of the change in GDP, show that on an actual output basis, the economy of the United States has been steady or declining since 1983. While it is quite possible to drive the price of something higher through greater speculation and more leverage, price is not equivalent to value. In the end analysis, you cannot grow value through borrowing, only through production.

Nobody in the media or government will talk about these statistics, despite the fact that the there's little room for argument on the mathematical facts.

There is an often-repeated line among various pundits that Clinton ran a surplus and that he oversaw the best economy in 40 years. President Clinton did no such thing. President Clinton, like all from Ronald Reagan forward, stole the Social Security and Medicare surplus funds and counted those funds toward the general budget, replacing them with IOUs from Treasury. While the Federal Reserve does not count those IOUs as debt, the fact remains that Medicare and Social Security are the third rail of American politics, and as of the end of 2010, there are $4.634 trillion of Social Security and Medicare IOUs in the funds' file cabinet. Until Congress admits that these forward promises to spend somewhere between $60 and $100 trillion in the future are never going to materialize and actually be paid out, we must count that $4.6 trillion as debt, because to spend it, it will have to become actual debt. Further, and far more important, all of the alleged great economy presidents in recent memory, including Reagan, Clinton, and then George W. Bush, did nothing more than crank debt in the economy to the sky to cover up what were in fact declines in actual economic output. Ironically, President George H. W. Bush, who is commonly thought of as a terrible president after reneging on his no new taxes pledge, actually managed a tiny net positive GDP on a four-year aggregate basis. President Clinton's performance, by comparison, was approximately negative 1 percent and George Bush's, on a debt-adjusted basis, clocked an astonishing negative 11.5 percent annually.

Maintaining the illusion of growth and expansion of wealth, upon which bubbles in the stock market, in real estate, and everywhere else rely, is why the debt chart shown in Figure 3.7 was allowed to expand. The imbalances we have run since the 1980s have been positively criminal. As can be seen in the total debt-to-GDP chart, the claim that the system has deleveraged, which is heard almost daily in the mainstream media, is a lie. All that has happened is that the federal government has taken upon itself some of the leverage that was formerly in the private sector. Very little actual contraction of systemic leverage, the total amount of debt outstanding compared with domestic output, has occurred.

The irony is that when one adjusts for debt, the recession was good, not bad. Our error was in attempting to short-circuit the contraction rather than allowing the market to correct the previous distortions. Recessions are supposed to bring the economy back into balance. As you can see from 1983 onward, the answer to all economic woes has been more debt, faster and everywhere, right up until we hit the wall in 2007.

The federal government and the Fed have, as Bernanke made clear, a thing called the printing press, with which the Fed can emit dollars without limit, either by printing actual currency or by creating new bank reserves electronically with the push of a button. Those new bank reserves then are allegedly to be used to generate more loans, that is, more debt. Many argue that this can be done without consequence so long as the reserves can be taken back out of the system when inflation warrants.

This is magical thinking. While it is true that one can emit dollars electronically or physically, the premise that one can repeal the fundamental laws of economic supply and demand while doing so is idiotic. Basic economic theory tells us that things have value only due to their relative scarcity. If the world contained as much steak as anyone cared to eat at any point in time, and no cost to produce an additional pound of steak, the price of each pound would be effectively zero. It is only relative scarcity of steak, and the demand for steak, that allows for the sale of hunks of beef. That relative scarcity for cut-up cow allows buyers and sellers in the market to agree on a price that compensates the farmer for raising the cow, the slaughterhouse for its work in processing the cow, the trucker to transport the meat to the market, and the store to package and sell that meat on the shelf.

When Bernanke emits additional currency via QE and other similar games, he is in fact debasing the currency. The price of everything denominated in that currency thus goes up, since the value of a unit of that currency, the dollar, expressed in terms of a bushel of corn or a gallon of gasoline, goes down.

With wages unable to rise due to global arbitrage, only two outcomes can result: Either the standard of living of everyone is damaged and they are able to spend less on discretionary items or the profit margins of businesses are squeezed as manufacturers cannot successfully pass through their costs by raising prices. Either outcome ultimately destroys the value of businesses and thus stocks, although both may appear to be recovering or even growing in the short term.

Intentionally cranking up debt higher and higher while decreasing the value of the currency must eventually fail, so why would a government engage in such a foolish practice?

Simply put, the government and Federal Reserve have backed themselves into a corner and are trapped.

Consider the debt-to-GDP graphs shown in Figures 3.4 and 3.6, and the income-to-debt-service chart from the beginning of the book. As debt increases, the only way to continue to make the payments on that debt is to have the interest rate go down. And what is the history of the Fed funds rate, the primary rate the Federal Reserve controls, since 1980? See Figure 3.8 for the answer.

That's a rather one-way chart. There have been ups and downs, but the peaks in interest rate have never exceeded the previous high since 1980. The reason is obvious: Without continually decreasing the price of borrowed capital, banks cannot support the loans they have made. Yet continually decreasing the cost of lent money, and thereby enabling greater and greater leverage in the financial system, is a suicidal game. Eventually, you reach a zero interest rate, as has occurred, and are forced to employ nontraditional tools like quantitative easing to keep the charade of systemic solvency going.

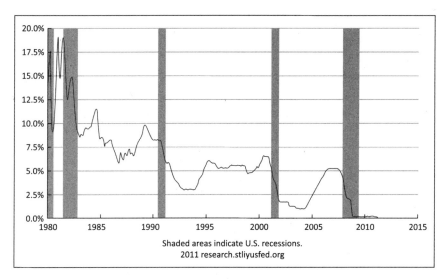

Figure 3.8 Effective Federal Funds Rate (FedFunds)
SOURCE: Board of Governors of the Federal Reserve System.

Should QE stop, interest rates will move higher. But there is a lot of debt out in the economy. The government itself has added more than $4.5 trillion of debt in the past three years. For each 1 percent move higher in interest rates, the government will have to come up with $45 billion in additional interest just on their borrowings for the last three years, and $145 billion annually on the entire debt outstanding. On the entire $53 trillion in current systemic debt, each 1 percent move higher in rates requires that the economy transfer more than half a trillion dollars each and every year to the bankers, simply for the privilege of keeping those lent funds active. To put this in perspective, that's about 3.4 percent of GDP that will be transferred from the real economy to the bankers for each percentage point move higher in real interest rates.

■ ■ ■

How did this sort of death spiral come about, and why didn't the government and the Fed see it coming and stop it? For the answer to that question, you have to think back to the basic premise of all exponential functions as outlined in Chapter 2.

Each loan that is made, no matter who it is made to, always occurs with intent to profit. No lender ever intentionally lends at a loss, and since there is always a risk of loss, the intended real rate of interest in any lending transaction will always be positive. But all loans rely on the forward ability of the person who takes the loan to pay from future economic activity.

This is an impossible combination for everyone in the economy to sustain, simply because the amount of interest required to be paid eventually must outrun the amount of money available. It is *inevitable* over a long enough period that some borrowers will not be able to pay and thus some lenders must lose their capital, just as it is mathematically inevitable that if you play the slots in Vegas for long enough, you will lose all your money.

This fact also points out the folly of government borrowing on any sort of long-term basis. A debt that is never paid down doesn't simply pay tomorrow for that which we need today. It in fact never pays for that which we cannot afford. Debt taken on in this fashion *mathematically must* destroy the person, entity, or government that does the borrowing. It is merely a function of how long a borrower will manage to deceive lenders into believing that the debtor will pay.

It would be nice if the problems were confined to the federal level. Unfortunately, magical thinking and the use of leverage to cover up incipient insolvency is rampant within the states as well.

The federal government can effectively print money. That's what happened with QE1 and QE2, despite Bernanke's claim otherwise. Borrow and spend as a fraudulent scheme is easier to keep going when you have a guaranteed straw buyer in the form of the Federal Reserve, which will suck up an unsustainable deficit and turn it into brand new cash. The fact that this action either must debase the currency and cause the price of commodities like corn, wheat, soybeans, oil, and cotton to skyrocket or must replace credit that was formerly issued and has now gone bad, thereby transferring real wealth from the citizens to the banks via a backdoor bailout, is simply disregarded. Indeed, if you look at the amount of deficit spending in excess of what the Bush administration ran from 2003 to 2007 over the three years from 2008 to 2010, you'll find about $3 trillion in aggregate,[17] and compare it against the decrease in financial firm credit outstanding over the same time (\$2.88 trillion),[18] you will find that the so-called stimulus spending by the federal government in fact actually almost entirely benefited large financial institutions by enabling them to cover up the enormous hole in their asset base that would have otherwise bankrupted them.

The states, however, cannot print money. The Constitution forbids states the ability to issue bills of credit, an effective prohibition on issuing currency.[19] The states have cheated the implied balanced budget mandate that comes from this prohibition in the same way people can cheat a cash shortfall for a period of time. The states borrow from tomorrow's tax receipts to meet today's needs, implying that tomorrow they will both be able to pay down the debt and meet the cash needs of tomorrow's state spending.

State and local governments have backed themselves into a corner by believing in the sustainability of home price appreciation. Using the increase in property taxes that they collected during the bubble years and projecting the same increases forward on an indefinite basis, budgets were drawn, government buildings expanded, and people hired. Yet the alleged expansion didn't come from true growth in industry and output in our nation, but rather from more and more borrowing by everyone in the country.

The most egregious abuses by state governments have come in the form of public pensions. These systems typically assume growth in their portfolios of somewhere around 8 percent. Yet going back to 1953, the first year Federal Reserve Z1 data were published, you cannot find a GDP growth rate that meets or exceeds those claims on any sort of consistent basis. In point of fact, the growth rate has been slipping materially for the last 30 years, as we have piled on debt throughout the economy due to the interest cost associated with that ever-growing pile of indebtedness. From 2000 forward, we have recorded an average GDP growth rate of just 4.2 percent throughout the economy in nominal dollars, while debt has grown at an average 7.4 percent over the same period.[20]

The correct response to our deteriorating economic situation would be to look at the reality of GDP growth and adjust expected pension returns to be somewhat less than that growth rate over reasonably long periods of time. With GDP growth of 4.16 percent since 2000, such a set of assumptions would leave pension plans with an estimated portfolio growth of about 3 percent net of expenses, instead of 8 percent. That change in expected returns would force pension funds to demand a much larger share of the employees' paychecks to fund pension accounts or severely curtail promised benefits. Of course, this computation does not take into account the sustainability of even the reported headline average 4.16 percent growth rate, as all the growth since 1983 has in fact been financed with new borrowing to maintain consumption. Properly adjusting expected returns to account for systemic leverage, one would be hard-pressed to argue that these pension systems could be made mathematically sound irrespective of the investment strategies they employ.

But instead of operating conservatively and facing the mathematical reality embedded in our economy, pension funds ventured into ever riskier asset classes to meet expectations, effectively doubling down on a bad bet. But with risk comes the possibility of loss. Investing in the stock market looks attractive with the often-advertised 11 percent annualized return, but distorting this historical average is a decade of extremely large returns from 1990 to 2000, approximately 400 percent across that decade or 15 percent compounded, that skew the numbers. From 2000 to 2010, the stock market has had no gain at all on a broad basis, and if you were in technology stocks, your account lost money. To expect on a forward basis that the stock market will return 11 percent annualized into the future on an indefinite timeline simply has no reasonable foundation, as such performance would represent a 184 percent increase in value every 10 years.

Hedge funds are even worse. Sure, hedge funds make a lot of money when things go well. But when a hedge fund makes a mistake, it often loses everything its investors put in. And hedge fund blowups happen far more frequently than anyone cares to admit. These funds are limited to accredited investors for a reason: People with a lot of money and assets are presumed to be able to lose a substantial part of their wealth without winding up in the poorhouse. But your average teacher, firefighter, and police officer did not accept these risks for their retirements. These individuals were told that their pensions were safe and invested in a prudent manner.

The claims of prudent investing without the risk of material loss and 8 percent or greater returns cannot both be true. In this regard, pensioners were misled, and that these funds were able to meet their targets for a while does not change the mathematical reality that there is no historical basis for a claim that people can both earn 8 percent or better on a long-term compound basis *and* have safety in their portfolio.

Public pension board members may be considered *fiduciaries*. A fiduciary is a person who is required to act in the best interest of the person to whom the fiduciary obligation is owed, in this case the pensioner. How can a public pension board in any state where this standard of care is imposed invest pension funds in vehicles that are exposed to significant risk of loss when the plan participants and beneficiaries are told, and reasonably expect, that the funds they were promised will actually be there when they retire?

The public pension system is broken. The alleged fiduciaries have not been held to their standard of care; they have been allowed to invest in various financial instruments that are dangerous and expose the pension fund to significant risk of loss. The pension plans have put forward expected growth figures, and modeled their portfolios and ability to pay, on asset growth numbers that have no basis in reality. Trapped by the laws of mathematics and the compounding of both growth and debt, pension funds are growing more desperate by the day, reaching for ever riskier asset classes in an attempt to claw back up the cliff that their fund balances have begun to slip over. This desperation plan won't work. While some pension funds may succeed through taking on additional risk, some will lose even more money or perhaps go bankrupt entirely.

If you're a teacher, a firefighter, a police officer, or other civil servant and have been promised a pension controlled by a state or local pension board, you need to look long and hard at whether your particular pension plan will be able to fund the payments you believe are due to you. States have tried to, and will continue to try to, game their way out of the trap these pension funds are in, whether by raising taxes, borrowing, shifting money around, or trying to invest in ever riskier asset classes. Some of the gambits undertaken by states will succeed for a while, but none of them can succeed forever. Raising taxes, such as the recent vote to raise Illinois's income tax by more than 60 percent, is doomed to failure since high-earners and corporations don't have to stay in a state where the tax burden becomes outrageous. Likewise, attempts to hold property taxes to the same number of dollars collected in the face of rapidly declining property values will only force property valuations down and ultimately cause even more people to default on their mortgages.

State and local employees were sold a bill of goods. As with all Ponzi schemes, everything appeared good until the need to actually pay the promised benefits escalated through the inevitability of compound growth. The only question remaining for most state and local employees is whether you'll collect your piece of the pension fund and die before the cash runs out or whether the fund is subject to some sort of forcible renegotiation of your benefits first.

Many state employees believe that the fact that their pensions are a matter of contract will protect them from an inevitable default. But a contract to do an impossible thing is no contract at all, under both common and statutory law. These pensions and their scheduled payouts over time, given the growth rate assumptions that are being used, are mathematical impossibilities.

Federal and state governments have contributed tremendously to illusory growth over the past two decades. Not only has our government allowed financial institutions and other corporations to record and post fictitious growth that was fostered by a debauched debt binge but also it constructed programs and entitlements that are absolutely dependent on the continuation of that charade for their funding. These schemes and artifices are mathematically impossible to sustain, leaving us only two choices as members of the electorate: a fundamental rethinking of what we can actually afford to pay for through the production of goods and services, or an uncontrolled collapse of not only the private economy but also governments.

Chapter 4

The Failure of Kicking the Can

In early 2007, the Asian markets suffered a huge one-day collapse that had no immediate and apparent cause. Examination of the first-quarter earnings reports of major banks, however, disclosed troublesome facts. Among other institutions, Washington Mutual, which has since failed, was paying dividends out of capitalized interest instead of cash earnings.[1]

The problem with the practice of paying dividends from something other than cash income is the uncertain nature of eventual collection of the funds in question. In fact, the only reasonable expectation Washington Mutual had of collecting the money allegedly due after paying it out to shareholders was if house prices were to keep rising.

But houses prices had peaked in 2006, especially in California, where most of their loans had been written. Regulators and the banks both knew these facts but continued to assume that home prices would rise in the future. Among the regulators who failed to act were the Fed, the Office of Thrift Supervision (OTS), and the Office of Comptroller of the Currency, all primary regulators for large banks and thrifts. These institutions were, collectively, the dog that failed to bark.

The response to the original collapse of the two Bear Stearns hedge funds in the summer of 2007 was predictable. The Fed cut the discount rate in August in a panicked attempt to inject more liquidity into the market. The intent of the discount rate cut, and the rate cuts that followed, was to make borrowing money easier. But the problem wasn't that borrowing money was too hard; it was that the funds lent out were uncollectible. You can't make a bad loan good by lowering the amount of interest owed if the person you lent money to has no ability to pay. All a rate cut does, in that instance, is delay the inevitable default.

The successive responses to ever-increasing amounts of financial stress by leaders worldwide has been refusal to recognize what happened, why it happened, and that political leaders themselves were complicit in, if not responsible outright for, the crisis. In fact, as late as July 21, 2008, just months before Lehman Brothers collapsed and panic gripped the market, Treasury Secretary Henry Paulson appeared on Sunday news programs and declared, "Our banking system is a safe and a sound one."[2]

But this time even lowering short-term rates to zero didn't stop the banking system from bleeding. In response to below-growth cost of capital from ever-larger amounts of liquidity, both governments and private entities had made loans without a care in the world for credit quality, allegedly selling off that risk to someone else and pocketing their spread. This sale, they believed, provided them a guaranteed profit. Those lenders then hedged by buying insurance in the form of credit-default swaps against the possibility that the person who was lent the money couldn't pay, but the writers of those contracts had no money, either.

The market should have imposed discipline against the outcome we saw in 2007 and 2008. As the financial system's leverage rose, the cost of insuring against a default should have gone up dramatically, choking off the alleged gains in home prices by forcing much higher interest rates to be charged to borrowers. In addition, market forces should have rendered unbacked writing of credit protection in the form of CDS and similar contracts unmarketable.

■ ■ ■

So why didn't the market work to prevent the concentration of risk and issuance of worthless securities?

The answer is found in the fact that the government allowed market participants to repeatedly lie and get away with it by backstopping them against losses. When Continental Illinois failed in the early 1980s, the Federal Deposit Insurance Corporation's (FDIC) decision to bail out bondholders began the destruction of market discipline. Later, during the Latin American debt crisis, Paul Volcker at the Fed once again acted to destroy the market's clearing function. Rather than force the reorganization of all the large banks that were insolvent, he intentionally ignored their bad debt to let them earn their way out of the hole.

These actions eviscerated market discipline, as there was no need for people in the market to analyze risk, nor was there any financial penalty associated with buying a bank-issued bond, even if the bank engaged in foolish lending practices. In short, the government decreed that those who lent capital to these large institutions did not have to pay attention to what these banks were doing with their money, as they would be protected from the consequences of making a bad investment. Through the 1990s and 2000s, this lack of discipline spread to literally every investment that was bank related or bank issued, including mortgage-backed securities and complex synthetic offerings such as CDOs.

Consider the case of the young man who first gets caught drinking while underage. Instead of having to earn his own money to pay the fine and face the judge alone, his parents show up to plead his case. The judge shows compassion. Six months later this same youth is caught driving while under the influence, and again the judge is lenient. Unless somewhere along the line this youth comes to believe that he will have to face the consequence of his actions, there is a high probability that he will eventually commit a serious offense. We then tend to argue that nobody could have foreseen this outcome, when in fact everyone involved had plenty of evidence that this young man was headed for disaster.

The argument for leniency and assistance lies in the premise that one learns through mistakes, and, if not permanently blemished, the offender can and will reform. This may be true in some or even most circumstances with youthful offenders of the law, but it is almost never true when it comes to corporate actors and government. Chief among arguments for this point of view is that since the 1980s savings and loan (S&L) crisis, executives have almost never been held personally to account on a criminal or even civil basis when their firms have imploded as a consequence of hiding losses. The Ken Lays and Bernie Ebberses of the world are few in number; out of the thousands of executives who put forward ridiculously rosy and unfounded expectations in their financial statements and business plans during the 1990s Internet bubble, only a handful went to prison or lost their fortunes. Yet the investors in firms that imploded during the 2000 tech wreck lost all their money. Our government's policy of refusal to prosecute even admitted criminal acts has not been confined to financial firms; myriad companies have admitted to felony violations of the law in various lines of business, including medicine and defense contracting, yet they have simply paid a fine.

In the 2007–2009 collapse, it was even worse. We have before us at the present time hard evidence that lending officers encouraged borrowers to lie about incomes to get mortgages; indeed, the lending officers were the only ones who knew exactly what the limits were in the automated computer programs that were evaluating loan applications.[3] We have, at last count, more than 150,000 withdrawn affidavits in foreclosure cases. In each of these instances, it appears that the person attesting to the correctness of the material in the document never read the paperwork. All of the large banks that were rescued got in trouble because they either made loans to people who had no ability to pay, relied on credit protection where the seller could not pay, or were writing protection they couldn't cover themselves, instead of making sound loans to people who were able to pay their debts. It has been alleged that some banks were putting together deals where the security was created at the behest of someone who expected a default, but the bank sold that security to others, representing that it would perform.[4] At IndyMac Bank, a federal regulator allegedly allowed the firm to backdate a capital infusion that made the bank's financials look better than they really were. That incident was particularly outrageous, in that the person at the OTS who permitted it was apparently also involved in the collapse of the Lincoln Savings and Loan in 1989![5]

Control fraud is behind most of these offenses.[6] Control fraud occurs when those in charge of an institution optimize the firm for the purpose of looting shareholders, creditors, and the general public. Control fraud is especially destructive when those involved in the management of the involved firms become intertwined with government functions that are seen as essential, such as the existing Treasury Primary Dealer network. Combined with the revolving door of government, these executives and their underlings wind up in government regulatory roles, where they can willfully avert their eyes.

A full litany of the sins of regulators and prosecutors in the form of intentional and willful blindness is well beyond the scope of this book. But the intentional refusal to investigate and prosecute wrongdoing among those who created the intertwined mess that emerged in 2007 and 2008 is an outrage that the people of the United States should refuse to stand for. The outright refusal to investigate and indict is nothing less than a declaration by our elected officials and those in law enforcement that they will not bring charges against those who intentionally harm the public trust and break the law, provided they work for a big, interconnected financial institution. This willful blindness is the formalization of control fraud as a legitimate business that, in effect, grants a license to loot.

Contrast this outcome with the S&L crisis, when more than 1,000 people went to prison for various forms of fraud, and many of them were top executives in the firms that failed.

We have seen trillions of dollars in economic damage done to our economy, most of it in the form of alleged appreciation of assets that never actually happened. Eight million people have been put out of work. More than a million foreclosures occurred in calendar year 2010. Our government has spent more than $4.5 trillion in borrowed money in a futile attempt to cover up and bury the intentional acts of those who looted the public during the housing bubble rather than expose and prosecute those responsible, sending the convicted to prison and recovering what we can to compensate those who have been harmed.

Congress has also been complicit in hiding the truth: Paul Kanjorski (D-PA) held a hearing on March 12, 2009, in which he literally *told* the accounting standards board, FASB, to change their rules for fair value accounting. He insisted that financial institutions be allowed to hold these assets at other than actual market value and made it clear that if the FASB did not do as he wished, Congress would legislate to force the desired change.[7] That hearing, almost to the day, marked the bottom of the stock market in 2009. Yet nothing material changed on that day in terms of the actual value of assets held by banks. Only the accounting treatment of assets was modified, and thus we changed how people viewed bank solvency, instead of actually resolving the underlying problem of loans that could not be paid as originally agreed.

We have not solved a thing by borrowing and spending this $4.5 trillion since 2008. All we have done is deferred and compounded the damage that our nation and economy must ultimately absorb before our markets will clear and the economy will truly recover.

Many in politics claim that we're loading a cost onto our children and grandchildren when the government borrows money. These politicians are delusional; not only are the costs impossible for our children and grandchildren to bear but also the current self-deceptions we are engaged in won't last another 10 or 20 years. We must deal with the excessive debt in our economy, or that debt will eventually force itself into the open and cause the collapse of both the economy and the political system of our nation. Thus far, however, that sort of candor has been astoundingly lacking in the corporate-owned media, with precious few exceptions.

■　■　■

One has to wonder how those who call themselves reporters can sleep at night. We've heard since early 2009 that the economy is recovering. But there has in fact been no recovery, as is easily demonstrated with facts and statistics from the very government that claims our economy is improving.

Let's first define the word *recovery* so we have a working basis to debate from:

> A general improvement in economic conditions for the population as a whole, including employment and wages adjusted for the actual cost of living experienced by the people, including any deferred costs that will be paid or expensed later.

The economic sector has been infested with people allegedly following the theories of John Maynard Keynes, most particularly in the past few years. These economists tout his theories as a tonic for what ails our economy. Keynes was famously known for his theory that government should act as a *countercyclical* buffer to the economy, and this has been used to justify the borrowing and stimulus spending that has taken place from 2007 to 2010.

The problem with this principle is the same as those who profess to be a Christian but take a black Sharpie marker to the Ten Commandments that proclaim that one must not steal or murder and subsequently go on a crime spree. Keynes's countercyclical theories likewise require not only stimulus spending when the economy flags but also increased taxation and running a primary surplus during years when the economy is doing well.

If you fail to put away funds for the inevitable downturns and spend as Keynes directs during recessions, the mathematics of compound growth bring catastrophe. Since both politicians and the people respond to an economic boom by demanding that government tax and redistribute less, the government never follows the more difficult half of Keynes's requirements. The best theory must be checked against human behavior, no matter how pleasant it may appear on paper.

Inflation is a funny word. In the common vernacular, it is the change in general price levels throughout the economy. The Austrian school of economics defines *inflation* as a change in money supply compared with economic output. That is, if the amount of money in the system increases faster than economic output, you have inflation, and vice versa.

It can be argued that a different definition is more accurate: *the rate of change of money and credit compared with economic output.*

Why the latter?

Pick up your wallet. Inside, there is probably currency, that is, dollar bills in some denomination. But there is also probably a collection of plastic debit and credit cards. The debit cards are equivalent to the entire store of your wealth in your bank accounts to which they're linked. That is, they're identical to carrying around all the currency you have in those accounts. But credit cards are a different matter.

A credit card gives you the ability to spend money you don't have. Through that spending, which you promise to pay for later, you expand the money supply exactly as if Ben Bernanke over at the Fed had printed currency and dropped it out of a helicopter. The same is true for all outstanding credit in the economic system in that it acts exactly the same as currency.

If we are to examine whether we have had inflation, we must therefore look at the change between both money and credit supply against economic output. Figure 4.1 reproduces the chart (Figure 3.4) from the last chapter.

The total debt-to-GDP ratio has been climbing rapidly since the early 1980s, reaching 375 percent of GDP at its apex, and it just recently took a small dip.

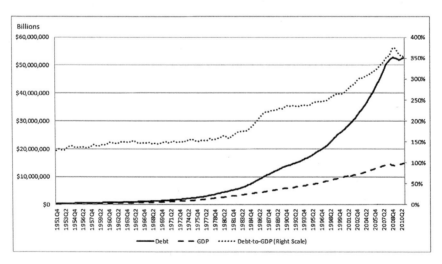

Figure 4.1 Absolute Debt to GDP
SOURCE: Federal Reserve Z1 and BEA GDP Series.

That's inflation in the monetary sense.

How much inflation? About 3 percent a year from 2000 onward, a bit less if you look from 1990. The problem with the expansion of credit as a driver of monetary inflation is that it brings with it the requirement to pay interest. This goes back to our foundational principles of two exponential curves and the fact that eventually you will find yourself unable to make those payments, since the required payments on the debt will always grow faster than GDP does.

The only way to stop the exponential cycle of debt is to contract outstanding credit so that the debt-to-GDP ratio comes back into balance with something approaching historical norms. This would require shrinkage of the total debt in the system by about 50 percent, a massive contraction that would undoubtedly bankrupt many lenders and borrowers. The resulting bankruptcies would ripple through to GDP as well, possibly contracting it by as much as 40 percent.

Now let's think this out a bit more. The gross debt in the system is about $52 trillion, give or take a bit.[8] It peaked, according to the Federal Reserve, at $52.788 trillion in the first quarter of 2009 and contracted to $52.38 trillion at the end of 2010, a reduction of some $408 billion in total. Yet we are told that the value of residential housing alone contracted by some $9 trillion over 2006 through 2010.[9] Where did that loss in value go, if it hasn't shown up in the outstanding debt number?

Where it didn't go is into defaults that were absorbed by the economy as a whole. That is, what didn't happen was a reduction in the total indebtedness in the system by that same $9 trillion. Nor have many of the defaults in the commercial real estate and general corporate area wound up reflected in the outstanding credit numbers, either. The government and Federal Reserve's actions have served to hide these losses rather than allow those who made bad lending decisions to suffer from them and for the defaults to be realized.

It's even worse when you look only at mortgages. The peak mortgage debt outstanding was $10.605 trillion in the first quarter of 2008. As of the fourth quarter of 2010, it stood at $10.07 trillion, a reduction of about $535 billion against the loss of value claimed to be some $9 trillion. While certainly some of the $9 trillion in lost value was lost equity—that is, it damaged the consumer's balance sheet—not all of that lost value can be explained in this fashion. Some of that lost value should have shown up in the banking and investment system in the form of impairments against loans that are no longer worth what they were collateralized with. In fact, only $535 billion has been taken off the balance sheets of financial institutions and the government on a collective basis. The rest of that lost value is being concealed through the use of additional systemic leverage.

That's not recovery; it's an intentional falsehood. The loss has been hidden, not written off or paid down.

Let's look next at employment. Remembering that nasty fact about compound growth rates again, we need to look at another factor when it comes to employment: Approximately 150,000 people a month come of age and are added to the ranks of the employed. Figure 4.2 shows the total employed number from 1999 forward.

Note that while there was indeed growth for a while in the total number of employed people, population has been growing at the same time. Worse, despite the claims of job growth in the last few months of 2010, you certainly don't see it in this series of data. The Household Survey says the job recovery peaked in July of 2010 and has been

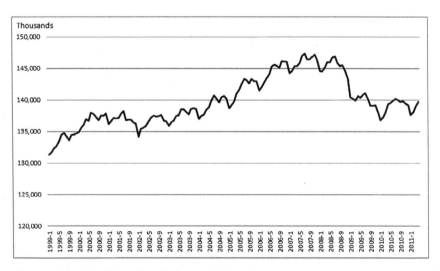

Figure 4.2 Total Employed, from 1999 to Present
SOURCE: BLS "A" Tables, May 6, 2011.

Figure 4.3   Employment Rate of the Population from 1999 to 2011
SOURCE: BLS "A" Tables, May 6, 2011.

bouncing along the bottom since. This graph also appears to show that while there was some job loss from 2000 to 2002, we had strong growth in employment right up until the end of 2007.

But that growth was in fact illusory, because population was going up at the same time. When we adjust for population growth, as shown in Figure 4.3, we get the employed rate of the population: the percentage of persons employed compared against the adult non-institutional populace. That table tells a different and disturbing story.

After a small upturn during the first part of 2010, the employment rate returned to its lows and appears to be also bouncing along the bottom. We also didn't see anything meaningful in terms of job recovery from the 2000 downturn when measured in this fashion, and we never regained the highs of 1999 we saw before the Internet bubble collapse.

If you're wondering how the expansion of leverage in the economy produced an apparent boom from 2003 to 2007 while average middle-class Americans saw their standard of living erode, your answer lies in this chart. There was, in fact, no boom at all. The entire claimed growth was nothing more than the expansion of credit and a resulting asset

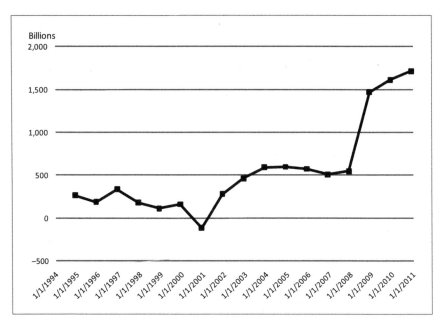

Figure 4.4 Federal Deficits Annualized, from 1993 to 2011
SOURCE: Treasury "Debt to the Penny" Series.

price bubble. We had very little improvement from 2001 to 2007 in the percentage of people who had jobs and thus contributed to the economy and to government via taxation. This should disturb you, given that the stock market from 2003 to 2007 was on an absolute tear in general terms, even though the Nasdaq never got much beyond half of where it stood before the tech wreck.

How can an economy truly expand when the number of people working in that economy isn't going up as a percentage of the whole? It can't, and in fact we cheated, as shown in Figure 4.4.

The last year of declining deficits was 2000. Since that time, we have run annualized deficits of around $600 billion from 2002 onward, right up until 2007, when they skyrocketed to $1.5 trillion and more. You can pretend to have growth by using credit. But it's not real growth, and it's not real wealth, because all credit must be paid back later, with interest.

This is where those who praise President Clinton for his alleged legacy of economic growth get it wrong. He had no actual economic growth, and neither did any president who came after him. The alleged growth was faked through credit expansion. Additions to GDP did not come from using output in the economy to pay for the goods and services produced, but rather through businesses and individuals taking on more and more debt to fund consumption.

It was a lie then, and it's a lie now.

Our government has provided an *illusion* of recovery. If you have a job and had one before, other than the ups and downs in the stock market, you probably haven't seen all that much change in your life-style. For the 8 million people who lost their jobs, it's a different situation. While it's true that the gross number of people employed had a small rise in the early part of 2010, that trend has now reversed. The job market has failed to recover, and when adjusted for new entrants to the workforce, as of the beginning of 2011, the percentage of people working is now bouncing along the bottom made in 2010. What's worse is that government's ability to fund itself on a long-term basis utterly depends on the employment rate of the population; without a meaningful recovery in that statistic, the hope that government will be able to increase tax revenues to ultimately reduce deficits is a fantasy.

We have responded to excess leverage in the economy by saying, "Charge it!" and in fact have increased leverage instead of allowing it to contract during the recession. We papered over bankrupt institutions by shifting some of their bad debt to the government, while we made legal holding bad loans on bank and other financial institution balance sheets at values that bear no relationship to reality.

The housing market has lost about 17 times as much in equity as outstanding mortgage debt has contracted. This is a travesty when one considers that a housing bubble was the cause of the economic col-lapse in the first place. Corporations may have record cash, but they also have a record lack of tangible assets and a record amount of debt, meaning that leverage in the stock market has skyrocketed rather than declined, as it should in a recession.

We probably shouldn't have expected our government to do any-thing different. After all, this is the same path that was followed when the economy got in trouble in 2000 and, in fact, in every recession since World War II to one degree or another. But as systemic leverage has built, the amount of distortion that the Fed and government have had to introduce to allegedly stabilize the markets and economy since 1980 has risen dramatically.

The all-in gamble of the government and the Federal Reserve has been to pump asset prices by increasing leverage in the economy as a whole, with hopes that animal spirits will take hold and somehow bring employment and demand back to levels that can support economic output. This is a losing bet, as it has been attempted twice previously in the past 30 years, and neither time was it successful. The reason the economy rolled over in the first place in 2007 was excessive leverage, as the cost of carrying debt had reached the practical economic limit; adding more is exactly like giving a drunk a case of whiskey and expecting him to be cured of his alcoholism.

The truth is that if the alcoholic doesn't stop drinking, he will inevitably wind up with either cirrhosis or liver cancer and expire.

If we don't change course in our economy, so will we.

■   ■   ■

Many have propounded what are alleged to be simple fixes to our economic system. Like all complex situations that arise in life, there are usually apparent ways to avoid the pain that look seductively simple. Unfortunately, they're usually wrong. The present circumstance we find ourselves in is no different, and no book on this topic would be complete without putting forward some of the most common purported solutions and then dispensing with them.

Hard money is one such belief. It is an often-repeated elixir for what ails us, and those who argue for it are fervent in their support. Sadly, they're incorrect.

What the hard money proponents are trying to eliminate is boom-and-bust cyclicality in the economy. We all love a great boom, just like many enjoy a good drink. But nobody likes the bust, just as nobody likes the hangover resulting from a night of overindulgence. Yet the two are interlinked, and, in a world where freedom has any sort of place among economic options, they cannot be parted, no matter what sort of machination we attempt to place in the way.

Let's assume for a moment that we have a hard currency, backed by gold at 100 percent. For each unit of currency, there is one troy ounce of gold in the treasury of the nation. Let us further assume that there are frequent audits to prevent anyone from playing games with the reserves, and thus we're quite certain that each unit of currency will remain backed by one ounce of gold at all times. We'll call this unit of currency a zotly.

Now let's assume that someone has managed, through hard work and industry, to amass 5,000 zotlys. Perhaps he has grown crops, manufactured toasters, or programmed computers. How he came by this mass of money in exchange for labor is not material, other than that he did so by the use of his hands and mind. That is, he produced a good or service of utility in the economy.

One day, while having a beer at the local pub, you come to this man with a great idea for a new business. You want to make and sell a new food, based on a slab of dough pressed flat and thin. You're then going to put some sauce, cheese, and meat on that slab of dough and bake it. You've even come up with a name for this wonderful creation: pizza.

But you have no money. The oven you need to buy, the storefront you need to lease, and the materials you need to set up your business all cost money. You're quite sure that you will make a profit selling these pizzas, but you lack the capital to get your venture off the ground.

You come across the first man, and he agrees to lend you some of his capital. You add up what you think you'll need to start your new venture and believe it will take about 2,000 zotlys for the first year. Your town's economy is not growing at the time, and there is no inflation either, but your venture remains somewhat risky. After all, the townsfolk might not like your new creation. While the lender can sell the oven if you fail and get some of his money back, the rest is going to figuratively go to money heaven if your business fails. So you agree that the man with the funds will lend you the money at 20 percent interest. You agree between the two of you that in one year you will pay him 2,400 zotlys.

You can see where this is going. Since in your economy there is no growth going on, the lender priced the loan accounting only for risk and not for monetary expansion. But the other 400 zotlys don't exist right now in the economy, and they won't in a year. The only way you can pay the lender is by managing to collect some of the existing money from everyone else in the village. That sounds reasonable, as you're providing a new product that didn't exist before, and you're quite sure your plan is going to work out fine.

In the first year, this sort of arrangement isn't much of a problem. But if you succeed and the lender collects the 2,400 zotlys and then lends them out, it eventually will become a huge problem. The reason is simply the exponential function. If there are a grand total of 20,000 zotlys in the village circulating, or any other number for that matter, the man who is doing the lending will eventually wind up with all of them, and everyone else in the village will be broke!

As soon as people amass capital they don't immediately need to spend on the necessities of life, they will seek to lend it out through one means or another. And as soon as they lend out that capital, the laws of compound interest rear their head. In fact, if we take our money and put it in a passbook savings account that earns interest, and let the interest accumulate, eventually all of the money in the world will wind up as ours.

A monetary system is in balance if the total amount of money and credit outstanding is constant when the output of that economy is also constant. That is, if there is no growth in the economy and the total of money and credit are constant, each unit of output in the economy can be purchased by a constant amount of money or credit over time. If the economy expands, to maintain balance money and credit must expand at the same rate, and if it contracts, likewise money and credit must contract. This is the premise of a hard currency. Since there is a limited amount of it, and it is relatively difficult to find or obtain more, there should be an increased level of stability.

Such a premise fails, however, because those who have capital have every right to lend it to someone for some purpose, and they always charge interest. As soon as that happens, we're right back where we started.

If the economy expands rapidly, there will be great additional demand for money. This will in turn spur people's desire to dig for more of whatever that currency is backed by, in this case gold. But the ability to produce gold lags the expansion in the economy quite severely because it takes time to dig up the ore, separate it, refine it, and process it into coins or deposit it as backing for the issuance of some sort of talisman, such as paper banknotes backed by gold bars. During that time, the economy is expanding, but the money and credit supply are not, and as a result, the economy suffers severe deflation. This in turn causes those who borrowed to have to pay with money that becomes scarce, and the value of their debt in terms of economic output goes up.

This action ultimately chokes off expansion in the economy, and we have a downturn. But the folks digging up the gold don't stop attempting to do so instantly. Now the new supply of money floods the market while the economy is receding from all the people who couldn't pay their debts and ended up going out of business. We thus have uncontrolled inflation.

History bears this out, and it also demonstrates that when you have a hard currency, you have just given the people who own that resource, such as gold mines, an enormous amount of power. Those who have control over a small resource can cause inflation and deflation at will by either holding back or flooding the economic system with their commodity. Those people can and will do so, first inflating the money supply to make it seem that credit is very easy and reasonable to obtain, and then pulling the rug out from under those who are foolish enough to take loans through intentional deflation. The bankers ultimately seize all the collateral that was pledged for those loans and throw the people into the street.

If you look from colonial times in the United States to now, you'll find that before the Federal Reserve, there were tremendously disruptive bouts of inflation and deflation, and in some cases, the change in the value of a dollar in terms of goods and services reached 20 percent or more within a single year's time. It is true that the average value of a dollar from the start to the end of that period did not change much, but you don't live your life in a manner that allows you to cherry-pick the start and end dates of your monetary experiment. Instead, you have a time when you want to get married, start a family, build a business, and plan your retirement and a time when you ultimately expire. Changes in the value of the currency over short periods of time leave you with a terrible choice. If you borrow to buy a home or build a business, only to see the value of the currency rise 20 percent in the next two years, there's a fairly decent chance you won't be able to pay and will become bankrupt, simply from the deflationary pressure and not from whether you made a good or bad economic decision.

The real problem in all economies is the lending of capital with interest and the inherent leverage and compound function this introduces into the economic system. Attempting to grow credit and money to meet the demand of interest due on lent funds inevitably must, if continued on an indefinite basis, result in runaway inflation and destruction of the currency. Failure to do so must result in recession and in lender and borrower bankruptcies. This requirement for economic balance is a constant, and whether you're living with a hard or fiat currency system is immaterial.

Hard money doesn't solve the problems we face and in fact introduces new ones. Those advocating for this change are mostly individuals with glimmers of instant wealth in their eyes. Some have even claimed that the fair price to convert the U.S. money and credit stock to gold would be in the $20,000 per ounce range or more. The first question to ask someone who wants to return to the Gold Standard is "How much gold do you have, and will you forfeit all of it, without compensation, to get the gold standard you want?"

Make sure you duck when asking that question.

■ ■ ■

Next we must deal with the often-repeated mantra from Ben Bernanke and others in central banking and economic circles who have repeated that a 2 percent inflation rate is what a monetary and economic system should strive for. Indeed, Bernanke has often argued that this rate of inflation defines "stable prices."

He's wrong. In point of fact, the common and expected state of any economy over time is a mild deflation!

Deflation, in the common definition within economics, is a pervasive decrease in the general price level in the economy. Yet that is exactly what we all seek and what, through the promise of technology and advancement of human productivity, we find.

Consider just a few examples. The original personal computer available for retail sale was the MITS Altair 8800 in 1975 and, shortly thereafter, the Apple II and TRS-80 Model I. Today, for less money than you would have spent on any of those, you can have a fully functional machine that is more than a thousand times faster and stores millions of times as much data. The original pocket calculator introduced by Monroe in 1972 cost $269 and was approximately the size and weight of a common brick. Today, you can often find solar-powered models that perform the same functions and are roughly the size of a credit card for a couple of dollars at Wal-Mart. The first VCRs cost over a thousand dollars but quickly fell to a few hundred dollars in price, and the first portable CD player, manufactured by Sony as the Discman D-50 in 1984, sold for several hundred dollars. That price did not last long either, and today a portable CD player sells for under $50.

The original RadioShack cellular mobile telephone sold for $1,200, weighed 10 pounds, had a carrying handle, used two six-volt sealed lead-acid batteries for portability, and provided about an hour of talk time when not plugged into your car. Today, you can buy a cell phone with more features and functions for under $50 that is the size and weight of a candy bar.

The advancement and natural deflationary tendencies in an economy are not confined to high-tech devices. The automobile was monstrously expensive until Henry Ford came up with modern assembly-line techniques, allowing him to build a Model T in 93 minutes. The price of automobiles immediately plummeted. The microwave oven was first introduced to homes in 1955 by Tappan, priced at $1,295. Today a microwave oven can be had for under $100; in 1955's dollars, accounting for inflation, you would have paid $12 for that oven or a mere 1% of its introductory price!

At its core, the drive toward deflation in an economy comes from improvements in technology and human efficiency. We call this an improvement in productivity. We find better, faster, and cheaper ways to do the same things that once were done with raw human labor, and in doing so, we are able to produce goods and services with the expenditure of fewer resources. We once spent most of our days hunting and gathering food, along with repairing our simple straw huts and developing other means of keeping out of the elements. Humans then discovered that they could domesticate animals, allowing them to work more land with less time and produce more with the same effort. We next figured out how to make machines that were more efficient than animal power, and again, we learned to produce more with less effort. This continual advancement in understanding and technology has driven the human condition. Today we enjoy flush toilets, electric power on command, automobiles that travel thousands of miles without significant maintenance, jet airplanes that transport us for a few hundred dollars across the country, mechanical refrigeration that keeps food stored at home safe for weeks at a time and more.

All of this improvement in our standard of living is deflation in action, and its power is almost entirely responsible for the advancement of the human condition over the millennia. When someone like the Federal Reserve's Ben Bernanke argues that 2 percent inflation is consistent with his statutory mandate, he is actually arguing for *destroying* wealth and progress among the people at large, literally stealing productivity to enrich a favored few among his associates. Indeed, in 2002, Bernanke presented a paper titled "Deflation: Making Sure 'It' Doesn't Happen Here."[10] In that paper, he argues for the monetary authority to step in and force a decline in the standard of living by causing inflation, when the natural order of human innovation leads the economy to produce exactly the opposite outcome!

The justification raised by those who argue against allowing the natural course of deflation is that it makes debt harder to repay, since the marginal value of each unit of currency goes up. That's a feature of a properly operating economic system and is not to be discouraged. One should not borrow in the general sense to consume or to speculate and certainly not with the only hope for a profit being a bigger sucker appearing to take your purchased asset at a higher price. Indeed, precisely the opposite is good for the economy and maintains its balance. Those who borrow or lend foolishly should find themselves in distress or even bankrupt. Bailing out both borrowers and lenders who were all well aware of the natural deflationary tendencies in the economy and profited from them for years is not only foolish but also destructive to people's ability to innovate and enjoy a better life.

There are only two ways to manage the inescapable mathematics that govern our economic system. First, one can bar, by law, any sort of lending at interest of any kind. To be effective, this has to be backed with the use of force, because it is not sufficient to restrict lending by banks or limit the interest rates charged. Since people always seek to make a profit in any economy, they lend only if the rate of interest they can charge compensates them for the four essential elements of any such transaction: the risk that you will not pay, the time value of money, the risk of currency debasement, plus a profit. The cost of money will always exceed the rate of long-run growth in the economy, and any attempt to limit interest rates charged to less will cause lending to cease.

This leaves only one other option: Admit the inescapable need for recessions and accept that not only are they necessary but also they are to be encouraged, and no amount of government intervention should be attempted or employed to blunt their impact.

Recession is the only way one can bring the debt and GDP numbers back into balance. Periodic recessions bankrupt both borrowers and lenders. Borrowers who became overextended cannot pay and lose their assets, which are then sold off, while lenders who made loans to people who can't pay lose some or all of their capital. This removes both the credit and the debt from the economy. It stops asset bubbles in their tracks, because the overleveraged assets are lost by the person who bought them using too much leverage. Those assets are then marked down to whatever the market will bear and resold, establishing a clearing price. It stops stock market appreciation that goes to wild multiples, because the risk of that leverage collapsing without warning is ever present, and without the unspoken promise to bail out markets, capital flows dry up as speculative leverage rises.

We have spent 30 years without any meaningful contraction in total economic leverage throughout the system when we compare debt and GDP. Prior to the 1980s, market forces imposed by recessions caused corporations that were unwise in their use of debt to pay the price as recessions wiped them out, and the buildup in ever-increasing leverage didn't occur. We oscillated between a corporate leverage ratio of somewhat under 1 when stocks were a good buy and right around 1.5 during periods of speculative fervor, when one could argue they were a sell. The 1968 peak in leverage brought a major sell-off in the stock indexes, and the 1972–1973 peak in leverage brought a loss of 50 percent to stock investors, with the old index highs not recovered until 1980. Most important, however, was that during this time corporations built true value in their balance sheets with little debt, preferring instead to attract investors with plenty of assets, dividends and cash. When you bought a stock in that era, you bought actual ownership in real things, whether they were cash, property, plant, or equipment, rather than ethereal promises of better ideas.

The 1980s featured Continental Illinois, the Latin American debt crisis, Long-Term Capital Management, and the Asian debt crisis. From those events, a tectonic shift became evident in both the Federal Reserve and Congress. The chosen resolution to all of these events was to bail out those that were too big to fail, with no meaningful restrictions on their conduct. To cover up the failures, markets were goosed to encourage taking on even more debt. The 1980s debt binge engaged in under Paul Volcker's time at the Federal Reserve set the table for what would be attempted when technology stocks collapsed and 9/11 occurred. The continuation of these unsound practices ultimately led to the housing bubble and the collapse of 2008.

The modern leverage era began in 1984 with the failure of Continental Illinois Bank. A bank that was founded in 1910 and had survived the Great Depression, Continental Illinois purchased bad loans from the failed Penn Square Bank of Oklahoma under dubious circumstances. Continental Illinois was deemed too big to fail by the FDIC, and bondholders were protected from loss, which went well beyond the official mandate of the FDIC to protect depositors. Similar to the 2008 bank rescues, the government acquired a large chunk of the bank and then sold it off later. Ironically, when the bank was resold into the market, it was Bank of America that purchased the majority of the assets.

It is no accident that coincident with this rescue, the debt-to-GDP ratio in the economy took off on a tear, never to look back. By declaring that those who lent money to a large financial institution would not suffer from its failure, our government declared that there would no longer be recessions that rippled through the lending of capital and stung those who did so inappropriately. The result was clear, convincing, expected, and obvious: The ratio of debt to GDP in the economy as a whole more than doubled over the next 25 years, and total systemic debt outstanding went from $7.4 trillion to $52.3 trillion, a 600 percent increase.

We have accomplished nothing good through this practice, and despite the claims by legislators in enacting the Dodd–Frank Financial Reform Law, nothing has changed. The large institutions that were too big to fail in 2008 are now larger and just as interconnected, and they present the same risk to the financial system from failure that they did in 2007. Despite provisions in the law that provide authority to pre-emptively break up any institution that poses systemic risk, not one bank has been broken up prospectively.

Some of the worst lending abuses we saw leading up to the collapse in 2008 are back. There are already reports in late 2010 and early 2011 of people with multiple late payments on their mortgage or credit cards being given single-digit interest rate loans to buy new cars, with no down payment, by too big to fail institutions that were rescued by the government. There are parts of the nation, especially the Washington, DC, area, where the ill-fated ARM mortgage option has again been made available, in an attempt to restart the housing bubble. Many Home Affordable Modification Program (HAMP) mortgage modifications are in fact balloon notes, which are the exact mortgage structures that blew up in the 1930s and cost so many Americans their homes.

Many in the economic realm claim that we should and can moderate or prevent recessions and that steady and appropriate economic growth can be maintained in perpetuity. These people, whether politicians, central bankers, or economists, are fools at best. They are making claims they know are false. Either the growth of credit and money in the economic system, including all interest owed, must be no greater than growth in GDP, or you will produce inflation in some form. That inflation may take the form of an asset bubble or the intentional destruction of purchasing power on the nation's standard of living, but it is mathematically certain to occur. No amount of central control can change this fact, and the more government attempts to distort the market, the more extreme and damaging these manias and collapses become.

Financial institutions that are too big to fail are too big to exist. There are already laws that criminalize threatening the government with its destruction. A threat of martial law[11] appears to be a per se violation of those laws. The mere concentration of financial power to this degree is by definition such a threat and is unacceptable to a free people and republican form of government.

■　■　■

It certainly would be nice to figure out a way to avoid recessions and the necessary creative destruction that comes with them. However, mathematics does not provide a way to avoid the need for periodically bankrupting some percentage of both borrowers and lenders so the two exponential curves that inevitably result from lending at interest can be brought back into balance. Those who argue that this outcome is somehow unjust are nothing other than tyrants in that they seek to protect themselves from their folly by stealing from everyone else. There is no requirement for you to engage in lending or for you to borrow another's capital. All these individuals and firms are doing is arguing that the common good requires that when lenders do something stupid, the lender should be able to force society as a whole to bear the cost of that foolishness, while the profit from good decisions remains theirs.

Recession is not to be feared. Those who are the weakest economically or who make bad decisions must be allowed and even encouraged to fail. Those who use debt as a means to finance speculation and consumption must feel the bite that comes from this demonstrably unsound practice. A free society does not proscribe the actions of those who live in it, but it does require that those who engage in dangerously unsound financial practices must bear the costs, including but not limited to their bankruptcy.

The mathematical facts make the conclusion clear and inescapable: It is only through the default of weaker credits in the economy on a periodic basis that economic balance can be maintained and—when imbalances have built up to the ridiculous levels we see today—restored.

Part Two

A WAY FORWARD

Chapter 5

The Folly of Avoidance

Normally in a book of this sort you would find a discussion of how you can shield yourself from the certain-to-occur disaster. Some authors would advise you to buy gold, others to invest in foreign currencies, and still others to engage in a diversified strategy involving common stocks, bonds, and currencies across the globe, along with various commodities.

You will find no such recommendations here, for the simple reason that none of these strategies will prove effective to protect your wealth if our society does not change course. If you are one of the few who has the ability to pull on the levers of power in government, you might be able to become a pick-and-shovel seller in a sea of ever-increasing and unstable pyramid schemes. But unless you can amass billions and disperse it all over the world—and have the means to get to any of those locations on a moment's notice and abandon those assets in places inhospitable to you—it won't matter.

The issues we face as a nation are not limited to the United States. Since the dollar is currently the world's reserve currency, if we hit the wall in the United States, economic repercussions around the world will be extremely severe. Becoming an expatriate may appear alluring, but it is fraught with danger; foreign nations are likely to become extraordinarily hostile to Americans, should we cause *their* economies to collapse as a result of our foibles. Large amounts of money can buy security, but do you really wish to live behind a barbed-wire fence and 10-foot-high concrete wall for the rest of your life? Travel to Jamaica and drive a few kilometers away from the tourist traps where cruise lines come into port, and you will see exactly what sort of fortress-style structure you will have to construct to be reasonably secure.

Likewise, if you follow the advice of many to buy gold, and the dollar collapses, you might believe you have successfully sheltered your wealth. Nothing could be further from the truth. While the government is unlikely to again attempt confiscating gold as it did in the 1930s, it is trivial to slap a 95 percent capital gains tax on the metal and demand that you document your purchase price for tax purposes. If the government takes such an action, your stash of $10,000 per ounce of gold turns into $500 in your pocket. The choice to deal in the black market will exist, but the risk of going to prison for tax evasion is hardly an attractive option.

For this reason, what you will find here are policy paths forward for our nation. These suggestions will not be painless for anyone in the Unites States, and there are powerful financial interests that align against all of them. They are designed to return the financial markets to a place that functions as a means of clearing payments while matching buyers and sellers, stripping the ability of various interests to blow Ponzi-style bubbles. They will require recognition of the insolvency of major financial institutions and government programs that have in fact been bankrupt for years but are trading on the premise of ever-increasing amounts of debt.

The core of where our economy is today and where we have traveled from has come about due to the Wimpy syndrome. We began by eating a single hamburger today that we promised to pay for next Tuesday. But then next Tuesday came, and we didn't have the money to pay for both the previously eaten hamburger and a new one for our empty belly. So we borrowed once again, and again.

All of this has pulled forward demand but has not led to actual prosperity. It has instead led to financial harm, as all borrowing comes with interest attached. The car we would have bought three years from now if we had saved was instead purchased today. Had we saved and waited the three years, our insurance bill would have been half of what it was, and there would have been no car payment. Yes, our car for those two or three years would have been scratched up and consumed a bit more gas, but it would have gotten us to work, and we would have spent the interest payments ourselves instead of giving that money to the banks.

The cell phone we bought on credit would have been purchased six months later, and we would have less expensive cellular service as well. We would have paid $600 for our cellular service over the last year instead of $1,200.

The college our kids are attending today wouldn't have come with a crushing cost that is impossible for any young adult to work their way through, consigning them to massive amounts of debt if they can't get an academic scholarship. The dorms would still be cinder-block buildings, there'd be a TV down the hall in a common room, and the awful food would be served cafeteria-style. But our sons and daughters could flip pizzas part-time to attend school, and they would still be learning calculus, computer programming, physics, or the practice of law.

Our houses wouldn't have ever cost $500,000 in a middle-class neighborhood. They would have cost $150,000 instead. Sure, they wouldn't have fancy granite countertops, measure 2,500 square feet, and be adorned with Viking professional kitchen appliances, but you'd be able to afford to buy one on a common $50,000 household income with one parent staying home and raising the kids. We'd probably have fewer teen pregnancies, gangbangers, and other miscreants for good measure, simply because someone would be there when Junior got home from school to make sure he did his homework.

We wouldn't have stolen the Social Security taxes in the 1980s and beyond. We could have decided in the 1980s to instead put each person's earnings into an account with their name on it. A true trustee arrangement, which many people think we have for Social Security but in fact never existed, could have been put in place. To do that would have required an actual zero inflation target that was enforced, and when the first signs of the leverage explosion showed up in the late 1970s and early 1980s, along with deterioration in the GDP/debt imbalance, that was the time to do it.

But we did none of these things. We chose to promise to pay tomorrow for the hamburger we insisted on eating today. We elected people to Congress who sang a great song about balanced budgets and fiscal responsibility. But as soon as they were elected, they did nothing but borrow and spend money we did not have. To make matters worse, they nodded pleasantly while the Federal Reserve and our banks abused the monetary authority vested in Congress by the Constitution.

Now the bill for more than 30 years of our economic, fiscal, and monetary foolishness is on the table, and the waiter is tapping his foot.

Our history is one of serially blowing bubbles in an attempt to evade the consequences of the previous collapse. In 1980, there was $4.4 trillion in total debt outstanding in the United States. In 1990, that figure reached $13 trillion, triple the 1980 figure. In 2000, systemic debt reached $25.8 trillion, double the 1990 amount. And in 2010, we reached $52 trillion, yet another double.[1]

The U.S. government debt has likewise more than doubled three times during the same period. In 1980, we had about $2 trillion in federal debt. In 1990, the total figure was in the $3 trillion range. In 2000, it was $5.7 trillion. And as of January 31, 2011, federal debt stands at $14.1 trillion. The Treasury Department has Office of Management and Budget (OMB) estimates that project another doubling of federal debt to approximately $26 trillion by 2020.[2] It is important to note that the OMB predicted a $5 trillion surplus in 2000 over the next 10 years, nearly extinguishing all federal debt. Instead of paying down that debt, we added $8.3 trillion to the total, so to characterize OMB's projections as unreasonably optimistic would be quite fair.

There is no chance that this next double will in fact take place. To do so even with a highly optimistic 3 percent interest rate would require the federal government to pay more than $800 billion in interest per year by 2020, paying down nothing in the process. In support of the alleged economic growth that is projected by economists, total systemic debt in the United States would have to double again to more than $100 trillion, and the World Economic Forum claims that on a worldwide basis an addition of more than $100 trillion is required in the next nine years.

Those who believe these sorts of increases in debt and corresponding interest expenses will actually happen are delusional. At 4 percent economic growth, a highly optimistic scenario allowing for no recessions and exceeding both last year's numbers and the projections forward on a durable basis, the economy will expand by only 48 percent during this same period of time. Yet that economy will have to support interest payments that are more than double their present level at the federal level and at least double what they are today in households and private business. Since excess leverage and debt service cost caused the 2007 economic downturn, to believe we can somehow manage to double once again the amount of debt in the economy while growing output by less than half of that amount is a fantasy.

If we do not act now, we will lose the ability to choose how to act at all. Our current economic path in this nation cannot be maintained. Blowing another bubble, which is what everyone in the government is desperately trying to accomplish, is doomed to fail. There has never been a nation in the history of the world that has managed to resolve being under the load of too much debt by taking on more, printing money, or tampering with interest rates. Each and every time the choice has been made to refuse to accept the truth, the price of fixing the economy in that nation has gone higher.

There are myriad examples of monetary and economic systems that have effectively or actually collapsed: Rome, Weimar Germany, Argentina, Zimbabwe. We are fools if we believe that it cannot happen here, because we are America.

It can and it will.

■ ■ ■

The path forward to economic stability will result in a contraction of GDP by 20 to 40 percent in the short term. This, formally, will be called a second Great Depression. Nobody wishes to use that phrase, and everyone in government claims we have avoided this outcome, which many spoke of during the dark days of 2008 and 2009.

But we cannot avoid this fate, as the die was cast 20 years ago or more. That which you put in motion and refuse to address for decades, you cannot prevent. The longer the United States keeps pretending and loading up on debt, the more damage the economy accumulates that will have to be absorbed.

There are arguments from the left side of the political aisle that we can raise taxes and close the budget gap. But a dollar you tax from someone is a dollar they cannot spend in the private economy. If such a decision is taken, then our economy will contract in size. Likewise, if we simply cut deficit spending as the political right pronounces, the economy will also contract. There is no way to avoid the arithmetic; we are spending money we don't have, and when we stop, no matter how we choose to do so, the economic activity funded by the borrowing that goes away will likewise disappear.

If we refuse, as a nation, to take our medicine and proceed down the path you will find in the following pages, there is only one piece of advice that can be offered and one safe investment that has a reasonable chance of success. You need to own enough arable land outright to raise a subsistence level of crops, such as vegetables and fruit. You need sufficient livestock, such as chickens and goats, to provide protein and milk. You need the skills to successfully raise both crops and animals. You need a way to produce sufficient energy for your own needs without the trappings of modern civilization and distribution. You need guns and ammunition, because plenty of people will try to take your crops and livestock from you by force. Finally, you need neighbors who will protect and defend each other, because no matter how well armed you are, there is always someone with more and bigger guns, and everyone needs to sleep.

Even assuming you manage all of this, it does not guarantee success. History is replete with nations that have gone through government and economic collapses. There is a high probability that should we undergo such a collapse in the United States, we will emerge with a very different form of government than what we have now—a government marked by tyranny and brutality, much like the Third Reich, where simply being of the wrong race, color, or creed could consign you and your children to death.

For the future of the United States, let's find a better way.

Chapter 6

Reinstating the Rule of Law

We all recognize that it is illegal to walk into a convenience store, stick a gun in the clerk's face, and say, "Give me all the money!" But when it comes to financial crimes, just getting the cases brought to court is a problem. The authorities prosecute a token offense here and there but refuse to bring criminal cases against the biggest institutions. The Expert Network prosecutions that began in late 2010 are one example of straw prosecutions to throw crumbs to the populace and make it appear that law enforcement is on the job. There have also been a few prosecutions where someone took out 20 mortgages and scammed a bank out of a few million dollars. Notably missing are indictments for the looting that goes on within the financial system itself, even when the evidence is nearly incontrovertible and in full public view!

This willful and intentional refusal to prosecute and enforce the law must end. Any institution that claims to be too big to fail is declaring its intent to use extortion to survive when it gets in trouble. When Joe Bank President or a Treasury secretary makes the argument that we must bail out some company lest there be tanks in the streets or riots, the correct response for Congress or the president is to call the sergeant at arms to lead that person away in irons.

We have plenty of laws to punish nearly all of the abuses that took place during the bubble years. It is illegal to sell a security to someone and represent you have received each and every mortgage in it, with all assignments completed by each party, if you really didn't. That's black-letter fraud, and when a financial institution is involved, it's a federal offense.

A loan officer who changes a client's income or asset declaration to meet a ratio test and then proffers that form back to a client for a signature commits fraud. If a loan is structured to meet conforming limits, and the structuring is done with the intent to deceive the ulti- mate buyer of that loan, that's a federal offense. The buyer who signs such a document is also committing a federal offense.

Richard Bowen, former chief underwriter for correspondent and acquisitions for Citifinancial Mortgage, testified under oath that in mid-2006, 60 percent of the mortgages purchased and sold were defec- tive under their guidelines. By 2007, that number had risen to 80 percent.[1] Not only did Bowen testify that the institution was making bad loans and selling them while fully aware that the loans were no good but also he documented communicating these findings to senior management. Knowingly making bad loans is a business decision. Knowingly selling defective mortgages to others without disclosing what you know about them is an entirely different matter.

An institution that puts together a synthetic financial instrument and misleads prospective buyers on how and why it came into exis- tence commits fraud. That institution induced people to enter into a transaction that they wouldn't have otherwise bought or sold by pre- senting intentionally false information, and the party they induced to invest lost money as a consequence.

Then there are all the other abuses that financial institutions engaged in, mostly by trading on their too big to fail status. The list is amazing in its breadth and length, including alleged and in some cases admitted money laundering for Mexican drug cartels,[2] transferring money to and from Iran while it is a black-listed nation,[3] and rigging municipal debt markets in various ways, from guaranteed investment contracts (GICs) to the sewer system in Jefferson County, Alabama.[4] In each of these cases, some individuals have been brought to justice, but the enterprise itself has not been prosecuted, even though the firm's involvement was necessary in some form for the act to be committed. It is hard to argue that the outsize profits received by this activity could have reasonably escaped the attention of management. The worst-case result for these firms has been the imposition of fines that amount to the ill-gotten gain, which makes the choice to engage in unlawful conduct a simple business decision. An institution that can engage in 100 improper acts, get caught in five, and simply pay a fine equal to the amount made on those five deals gets to keep the fruits of the other 95 infractions. If we imposed this sort of penalty on ordinary bank robbers, your neighborhood bank branch would be held up every afternoon.

This culture of corruption extends well into the Washington, DC, establishment. The long-existent revolving door between Wall Street and Washington virtually guarantees it. Can you realistically expect people who ran major Wall Street and Federal Reserve institutions to provide effective regulation and make referrals for criminal prosecution against the firms they once worked for or even chaired?

Professor William Black published a book in 2005 about the S&L crisis. His investigation of that crisis and the referrals that flowed from his activities produced more than 1,000 criminal convictions. In *The Best Way to Rob a Bank Is to Own One,* he put forward the model for corruption exactly as done in the 2000s.[5] Unlike the 1980s S&L scandal, this time it can be argued that these acts occurred with the near-explicit backing of the U.S. federal government and all 50 states. Not only has the Department of Justice and U.S. attorney general refused to prosecute any of these acts, so have the state attorneys general. Until and unless robbing the people is treated as a crime and those responsible are prosecuted and imprisoned, whether they wield a briefcase or a gun, we will never put a stop to the deceptions that have stripped and continue to strip the people of their wealth and economic freedom.

The season of the bankster must end. We, the people, must enforce our will on Congress. If that enforcement means ejecting every current member of the body and replacing them with a third-party candidate, then so be it.

■　■　■

Myriad laws allegedly govern the conduct of various agencies within the federal and state governments. For example, Prompt Corrective Action[6] is a body of law that requires the FDIC and OCC to monitor and correct the activity of banks before they get into enough financial trouble to fail. The purpose behind this law is to either force corrective action or, where it either can't or doesn't happen, to force the FDIC to seize the institution and resolve the bank before actual losses can occur to the deposit fund.

This law was ignored during the 2007–2010 period. We know this for a fact because in many banks that failed during that time, from the smallest to the largest, we have found that assets were carried on the books of the institution at prices from 20 to 40 percent higher than they were really worth. In some cases, these asset values were claimed in quarterly reports issued by publicly held banks just weeks before the failure happened. While rapid deterioration of value can take place, to believe that on a consistent basis a loss of 20 to 40 percent happened within weeks in virtually every case of seizure stretches credulity beyond the breaking point. What this pattern of events suggests is that the FDIC and OCC are simply ignoring the law and refusing to either mandate corrective action or close these banks until the losses become so massive that the institution can't pay the electric bill.

Likewise, in the case of Lehman Brothers, we discovered through the examiner's report[7] that market participants knew, weeks before they failed, that Lehman had no good collateral to pledge for their operating credit. The New York Fed also had to know this, since it was involved in clearing these overnight repo transactions on a daily basis. This information gave other market participants near-certain knowledge that the firm was bankrupt, but this fact was not widely communicated to the public. It is reasonable to assume that this inside knowledge was traded on, even though trading on material nonpublic information is unlawful under U.S. securities laws. The Fed was and is the large interconnected institutions' primary regulator, yet it did not raise any public alert about these facts, nor did the SEC, which allegedly regulates all public companies.

Why not?

In essentially every law bearing on the operation of a part of the government, even in the case of Prompt Corrective Action where the section of law in question is full of the word *shall,* there is no sanction for nonperformance or even intentional misconduct.

Consider how well the law against bank robbery would be obeyed if the sanction of prison time was missing. A law with no penalty clause is no law at all; it is a mere suggestion. The Federal Reserve Act of 1913 provides explicit limits on what the Fed can and cannot do with regard to its lending and asset purchase programs, and yet there is no penalty that applies if it exceeds that authority. Various programs like the Maiden Lane LLCs were set up during the crisis, and yet it can be argued that many were blatantly unlawful. The decision to engage in dodgy or even prohibited acts is easy to justify when there is no penalty that can be assessed.

Perhaps the most serious impact of all that arises from a two-tier legal system, where government and certain privileged entities are free to violate the law with impunity, is that it severely deters entrepreneurs from starting and expanding businesses. Every individual who starts a business understands and accepts the risk of losing to competitive forces; a competitor down the street or across the nation may be smarter, faster, or fortunate enough to discover a hidden inefficiency in the market and exploit it first. When recourse before the law is denied to small business, however, intentional and unlawful destruction of small businesses by privileged competitors becomes a risk that cannot be compensated for. If your competitor is able to access capital markets through misleading or outright fraudulent claims and thus can engage in a price war without caring whether they can fund their operations from revenues, you will lose your business due to their cheating. Likewise, if a Chinese firm can steal your intellectual property, duplicate your product, and then sell it and destroy your margins, if you have no recourse to the law, your business will be literally stolen from you.

Without small business, there is no long-term prosperity in an economy. Small businesses are the engines of both job growth and innovation. Microsoft, now a $200 billion corporation with thousands of employees, was literally founded in a garage. Thomas Edison and Alexander Graham Bell were more-or-less lone wolves; one gave us electric light and electrification of the United States, and the other modern voice communications. While large business interests do innovate, history has shown that many of the true advances in both science and technology occur through entrepreneurial activity. Destroying the incentives for people to personally engage in taking economic risks, stunts our nation's economy and severely damages its intellectual wealth.

■ ■ ■

One measure of reform we must take is to scrub federal and state law books and find all instances of strictures or prohibitions with no penalty clause. Those alleged laws are in fact nullities and must be struck, as they provide only false assurance against malfeasance and felony.

Once we have completed a full and complete review of the statutes at both state and federal levels, we can then debate in our legislatures about what should be reinserted into the statute books that govern the conduct not only of people but also of the government itself. During the ensuing debate on enactment of new laws, we must insist that any such regulation or law comes with an explicit penalty clause that provides a strong deterrent against violations, with penalties attaching not only to the government agency but also to individuals within that agency. Without addressing this shortcoming in the law, we will continue to see government agencies and employees act with willful and intentional disregard for laws that supposedly constrain their acts.

The refusal to impose punishment for willful blindness or even outright lies by government actors extends to the statistical publications our government puts forward.

Would you accept your electric bill if the number of kilowatt hours you used were adjusted to reflect some sort of government bias, but you were billed for the actual usage? How about going to the gas station, having the pump read 15.4 gallons, being charged for 15.4 gallons, but only getting 12.5?

Nobody would put up with an intentionally crooked gas pump at the corner station. But this same sin happens every month in government statistics related to the economy, and nowhere is it more outrageous than in the computation of the consumer price index (CPI) by the Bureau of Labor Statistics (BLS).

The government has a tremendous incentive to publish statistics that intentionally understate price inflation. Chief among these incentives are that many entitlement programs are indexed for inflation so that senior citizens and others who rely on them do not see a decrease in their purchasing power. But these adjustments are problematic in that they intentionally distort actual prices paid and they also attempt to include the utility value of certain products in the computation.

Utility, or hedonic adjustment, is highly controversial. An LCD direct view television is about 70 percent more expensive than a CRT or picture tube television of the same screen size, according to the BLS. Hedonics says that even though the LCD television costs 70 percent more, that price increase is not inflation because the LCD television has higher utility in that it both produces a crisper image and consumes less power.

That would be an appropriate observation if you could still choose to buy the CRT television. But in most cases, the older device is no longer made. So now your option, in the real marketplace, is to pay 70 percent more for the same functionality you had before or do without! While the hedonic model may say that there has been no inflation, in point of fact the day before the CRT television disappeared from the market, you could have bought one for $200. Now you must pay $340 to obtain what you had before.

Hedonics is often claimed to be most useful with something of basic need like a shirt, where the claim is made that a long-sleeve shirt has more value than a short-sleeve shirt, and thus some of the price difference should not be counted as inflation. The problem with attempting hedonic adjustment on shirts is that your opinion, even in the mundane case of a shirt, has much to do with the temperature. In the winter, you might consider a short-sleeve shirt to have a value of zero, while in Arizona in August a long-sleeve casual shirt may also have a value of zero. Attempting to square your actual circumstances with that of the BLS and its data is often impossible, yet this is exactly what the BLS attempts to claim it can do with some degree of accuracy.

The worst abuse, however, is related to housing. Here the BLS measures actual rental costs and something they call owner's equivalent rent. The former is straightforward and, assuming the data are accurate, leaves little to argue over. The latter is an estimate of what it would cost a homeowner to rent their primary and owned residence. This substitution for actual home prices dramatically and intentionally understated inflation during the housing bubble, because loose lending standards coupled with exotic mortgages such as option ARMs led to rent equivalents that did not rise at anywhere near the rate that house prices were increasing. Yet you, as a homeowner, actually paid for housing as an asset in terms of an obligation to spend the entire purchase price in dollars rather than rental costs, since your intent was to actually *own* the property.

This change to housing cost reporting was made in the early 1980s and is responsible for the CPI failing to pick up any of the housing bubble as inflation. Of course, we know that from a purchasing power perspective, the inflation in prices was very real, and in fact the lack of ability to buy using conventional mortgage products was a large part of what drove the housing mania. In addition, the intentional understatement of housing costs led to CPI numbers that dramatically understated the level of general price increases in the economy, and that, in turn, was used as justification for low interest rates by the Federal Reserve and economists.

Finally, the BLS weighting for the portions of the CPI is an average and is particularly unrepresentative for those of lower- and upper-end incomes.

The CPI assumes that the average urban consumer spends 15 percent of his income on food and beverages. Let's take a person who makes $18,000 a year, or $1,500 a month before taxes. Presuming they have only FICA and Medicare deducted—that is, they get back all of their income tax—they have $1,380 a month for income. This person's grocery bill is presumed to be 7.8 percent of consumable income, or $107.64. Primary shelter costs are assumed to be 32.3 percent of income, or $445 a month. Can you rent an apartment for $445 in a major city? Utilities are presumed to be 5 percent, or $69, including electricity, heat, water, and sewer. The CPI-U also claims 16.7 percent of income is allocated to transportation. That's $230 a month for your car payment, insurance, gasoline, parking, repair, and maintenance or for bus and train fares.

Is any of this realistic for the lower-income person?

The upper-income consumer is likewise distorted. The wealthy do not care much about food inflation since as a percentage of income, food is insignificant. Their transportation expense is almost all discretionary, as they buy luxury cars rather than basic transportation. And their housing expense may be close to zero if they paid cash for their home and thus have only hazard insurance and property taxes to cover as major expenses.

While it is hard to argue that absent these intentional distortions we would not have had a housing bubble, these knowingly bad statistics certainly contributed to the mania that enveloped the nation. In addition, this distorted view of the consumer price level is directly responsible for senior citizens and others on indexed programs of various sorts, along with lower-income people, being hit with a rapidly decreasing actual standard of living, while the government claims that inflation is contained or even nonexistent.

To make good economic decisions, we must have accurate statistics. It is vital that the BLS and other government agencies produce data that reflect what the consumer actually experiences in the marketplace. We have utterly failed in this mission over the past two decades when it comes to inflation. One of the most important parts of cleaning up our economic mess is to correct these distortions and put in place a mandate for accurate reporting, as seen by the actual consumer who is buying real products and services in the economy.

Chapter 7

Reforming the Fed, Lending, and Derivatives

The Federal Reserve Act contains the following in Section 2A:

> The Board of Governors of the Federal Reserve System and the Federal Open Market Committee shall maintain long run growth of the monetary and credit aggregates commensurate with the economy's long run potential to increase production, so as to promote effectively the goals of maximum employment, stable prices, and moderate long-term interest rates.[1]

Where in that passage do you see "stable prices" defined as "2 percent inflation?" Stable means, in the dictionary sense, "firmly established; not changing or fluctuating." Stable prices are essential to economic stability. When prices are increasing, actors in the economy are urged to spend money unnecessarily to avoid debasement of saved funds. The precise intent of the interventionist actions that have been undertaken from 2007 to 2010 is fundamentally dishonest for this reason in that it seeks to deplete savings and thereby destroy the foundation of capital formation.

It is essential to avoid distortions of this sort to remove the need for people to participate in asset bubbles, whether directly or via Ponzi-style proxies, to save for their retirement, for education of their offspring, and for their own personal needs and desires. Forcing individuals and corporations to either spend or invest savings lest they be debased creates speculation where it would otherwise not exist.

We often hear it argued that 2 percent inflation is a normal rate of inflation. This sounds quite innocuous, but in fact it is not. Remember the law of exponents and that you work, on average, from age 18 to age 65, or about 45 years. That is, your earnings at 18 are worth in real terms 2.44 times as much per dollar as they are on your retirement date with a 2 percent inflation rate over that entire period.

This makes the premise of saving for retirement a bad joke. You should be able to simply sock away 20 percent of your income and retire with reasonable comfort. If you earn a median $50,000 a year for 45 years, you will have earned $2.25 million. If you saved 20 percent of that income with no growth whatsoever, you would have $450,000. Assuming your home is paid for by that time, and remembering that there is no appreciation and thus no tax due on this accumulated wealth as it is pure savings, you could spend $25,000 a year for the next 18 years, allowing you to live to 83. Note that Social Security, if it was simply put away for you instead of being a massive accounting fraud, would be 13 percent of your gross income, meaning you would have to save just 7 percent on a personal basis to have a retirement fund good to your mid-80s. Further, your home, being unencumbered, could be sold or the value extracted as you age to provide a further income boost.

Who wouldn't like that system? This is what the Federal Reserve Act promises and has in fact promised since 1913. And it is what every Fed chairman from that date forward has *serially and intentionally* failed to deliver.

This failure is not an accident. Indeed, Ben Bernanke, our present Fed chair, doesn't even try to hide his intentions and those of his predecessors. He talks explicitly of the Fed wanting to see price inflation somewhere around 2 percent, even though that expressed intention is explicitly against the law. Congress does nothing about it, mostly because we the people refuse to take the time to understand how this compound function ultimately destroys our wealth over time.

The Fed's mandate, if we are to keep a Fed, must be rewritten so that price stability means what it says, and so there are serious sanctions for noncompliance. In addition, the targeted price level must recognize and adjust for the natural *deflation* in the economy that occurs through improvements in productivity and technological advancement. Debasement of the currency was originally punishable by 10 years in prison;[2] this seems an appropriate remedy and should be considered for reinstatement. A five-year rolling computation of the price level appears at first look to be reasonable, in that it allows for financial shocks and enforces a requirement to contract money and credit following inflationary periods and vice versa, while giving sufficient time to enact and enforce monetary policy consistent with a zero inflation goal.

There is another alternative, which is to abolish the Fed altogether. If we return currency creation to Treasury, getting rid of the concept of debt-based currency in the process, we would also get rid of government bond sales. There's much to recommend this path, and Representative Dennis Kucinich introduced a bill in 2010 to make this change, among other things, including terminating the ability of banks to lend on a fractional basis.[3]

But removing debt-based currency and government bond issues in favor of Treasury simply issuing currency to fund deficit spending is not a panacea. Kucinich's bill contains no provision to remove the excessive existing borrowing in the financial system, and in fact the bill attempts to protect those who would otherwise be bankrupted were that borrowing to become unsecured and uncollectible. Without debt-backed currency, the government's spending beyond taxing capacity in the present tense must be directly matched to economic expansion and private credit creation or destruction. If the supply of money and credit expands faster than the economy expands, there would be immediate monetary and price inflation. This means that deficit spending as we now know it could take place only during economic expansions. During contractions, government would have to spend less than it takes in via taxes. That is, the government might have to withdraw currency and literally destroy it, along with the recession's natural withdrawal of credit, to maintain monetary and economic balance.

Whether there is any hint of the discipline Congress would have to display to properly run such a system remains to be seen. The most likely outcome, unfortunately, is that Congress would make an exception for a short time when there was an economic downturn, and we'd be right back where we are today in relationship to credit and money imbalance. Without restraint, the nation could quite easily suffer hyperinflation or even a currency and political collapse.

To make a non-debt-based system workable, the same sort of sanction would need to be employed that could be leveled against the Fed and its price stability mandate. With Congress, there's an obvious problem, in that you're asking Congress to apply a sanction to itself for something it does, up to and including imprisonment of some congressional members. That's unlikely to work out very well.

What might work would be to vest monetary authority in some branch of Treasury with congressional oversight, as Kucinich's bill does. If there was both a mandate for price stability and criminal and civil sanctions, we might have a workable solution. The advantage to this system over what we have now is that there would be no interest expense to the federal government, which would reduce government spending and thus the need to tax over the years by literal trillions of dollars. The bankers wouldn't like this change as they're largely the recipients of those interest dollars. But this system would present an automatic balancing force on the budget if sufficiently strong sanctions were to be part of the law in that if Congress or Treasury tried to run a deficit beyond growth in the economy, people in the executive branch would go to jail.

If there's one thing to recommend such a change, it's this: There would be no question about who was responsible if the monetary and political system were to be destroyed as a consequence of willful refusal to follow the law.

■　　■　　■

Whatever decision we make as a nation on the presence or absence of a central bank, and however we denote the monetary authority, there are a few points we must address. First, the debt-to-GDP ratio must come back into balance with historical norms. Rather than set explicit targets, however, the best means for forcing the necessary adjustment to happen is to make lending money for speculative or consumptive purposes expensive. Allowing natural deflationary forces in the economy to come to the forefront will go a long way toward this goal.

In addition, there must never be a real negative rate of interest so long as there is provision of liquidity by whoever holds the monetary authority. Paying people to borrow always winds up producing a speculative asset bubble and subsequent bust. This is simple human nature in that if you pay someone to do a thing, they'll do a lot of it. If liquidity is always moderately tight, even during economic downturns, then it only makes sense to borrow for productive purposes. Borrowing for consumption or speculation—much less to find a greater fool—becomes expensive and risky enough that it is simply not worth it except in extraordinary circumstances.

We can fix the Federal Reserve or we can abolish the Federal Reserve. What we can't tolerate in our economy is a Federal Reserve that decides that 2 percent inflation is their interpretation of the clear English word *stable*. This act, standing alone and unchallenged for nearly 100 years, has done more economic damage to the United States through both direct and indirect effects than all other harms combined.

Most of what happened during the housing bust, and all of what happened leading up to it, can be traced to one thing: the ability of banks and other financial institutions to issue infinite amounts of credit money without backing those loans with anything at all.

This is a power that allegedly belongs to the sovereign. In fact, in the case of the United States, this power is explicitly in our Constitution, in the form of Article 1, Section 8, which states that Congress shall have the power:

> To borrow money on the credit of the United States;
> . . . .
> To coin Money, regulate the Value thereof, and of foreign Coin, and fix the Standard of Weights and Measures;

These powers belong to nobody else, and since credit and currency all spend the same, one who lends against nothing is in point of fact creating money. That, by the black letter of the Constitution, is forbidden without explicit congressional authorization.

Yet this is what banks do every day when they lend money in an unsecured fashion. This lending inevitably produces monetary inflation, since money and credit both spend exactly the same. That inflation in turn drives an asset bubble somewhere, which leads people to borrow even more to chase expected profits. The banks dutifully skim off commissions and fees while claiming they're just performing the service of making a market and denying that it is their lending activity that leads to the speculative fervor in the first place.

When the inevitable collapse occurs, banks find ways to avoid eating the consequences of their bad decision making. Indeed, the banks profit again, this time by foreclosing on homes and adding late fees and penalties to the very unsound loans they initiated in the first place. They manage to do all of this even though from the beginning of the cycle, they were operating with superior information and knew in advance exactly what would happen, even if they weren't sure exactly when.

■ ■ ■

There's a better way.

If banks can lend against only either hard asset valuations or their own capital, then the boom-and-bust cycle cannot take root. Let us presume you wish to borrow to buy a $20,000 new car. The vehicle depreciates by 20 percent when you drive it off the lot. The bank can thus finance, based on the asset value of the vehicle, no more than $16,000. If the institution wishes to write a loan for more than $16,000, it must have its own capital behind the rest of the loan. In addition, the bank cannot write a loan that enters negative equity at any time during the loan's term unless it has actual capital behind that negative equity position on a dollar-for-dollar basis. The bank could, if it wished, sell bonds to the public and, with the bondholders' money, fund the other $4,000. But the bank's bondholders are now the ones who lose if you don't pay on your loan. If the car is seized and resold, and $16,000 is recovered, the $4,000 is lost, and that loss is directly charged not to the public through a bailout, but to the bondholders.

Combined with a fixed reserve amount of 6 to 10 percent of all assets that must be held in cash to allow for the possible rapid loss of collateral value, there is no systemic risk or depositor loss that can arise.

Trade in derivatives, which are backed by nothing, and unsecured lending such as credit card loans would have to be fully reserved. That is, for each dollar of such an exposure, the bank would have to obtain one dollar of retained earnings, bondholder capital, or shareholder capital. Banks that wish to grow would have to attract either bondholders or shareholders and could not use deposits covered by FDIC guarantees. A customer who wished to invest with the bank could do so in a CD-like instrument, but that investment would be entirely unprotected against the possibility of loss. Non-interest-bearing transaction accounts, such as checking accounts, would remain protected by FDIC insurance.

If the bank's asset values declined, then the bank would have to come up with additional capital, dollar for dollar, against that now-unsecured debt or sell the asset when its market value reached the amount of the indebtedness outstanding.

With this as the model for banking and lending, there is never systemic risk, and a bank failure can never cost a depositor or the deposit insurance fund any money. That is not to say that people can't lose money under such a system. Banks can and will go bankrupt, and the shareholders and bondholders who were underwriting the unsecured portion of the bank's portfolio of assets will take losses, up to and including possibly being wiped out.

Such a set of requirements turns banks into effective utilities. But this status is inherent in the function they perform in the first place. A bank is an edifice established by governments to lubricate commerce by matching persons with capital with those who wish to borrow, clearing financial transactions in the ordinary course of commerce, and temporarily storing funds in a safe manner for customers. Speculation and various other business schemes have their place in the economy, but they must not be intertwined with the essential function of clearing transactions in commerce and safekeeping consumer and business money.

The risk in this design on a systemic level, as opposed to individual investment losses, comes from regulatory malfeasance, not bad luck or economic downturn. For this reason, the FDIC backstop must be maintained to protect against the failure of government to act as required, but structures must be put in place to minimize the risk and make fraud unprofitable. The simplest way to do so is to force the exposure of all asset values and portfolio components in real time to the public and insert a strong penalty clause into the Prompt Corrective Action[4] section of existing federal statutes.

Coupled with a return to the rule of law with regard to frauds, we need never again have a systemic banking crisis or the sort of outrageous serial speculative asset bubbles we have just witnessed twice in the last decade.

There are many who have argued for the reinstatement of Glass-Steagall. It's not a bad idea. The original law was a mere 17 pages of very clear legislative text. But "one dollar of capital," as presented previously in discussing banking, both goes further and shuts down all the schemes and risk hiding that banks can engage in, making a bank an effective public utility, while retaining private ownership of the financial system. Whether a bank takes deposits under this standard becomes immaterial, as deposit-based lending cannot happen on an unsecured basis.

■ ■ ■

There are few possessions closer to the heart of Americans than their homes. Financing the purchase of those homes has been a necessity ever since we started with planned urban development and similar schemes. The colonial era practice of acquiring 160 acres of land, building a small lean-to on it, and then adding piecemeal over time is long past.

Our existing system of household finance, however, is terminally broken. Housing finance can be fixed only if we stop looking to the government to solve every problem through some sort of backdoor game and instead return to a straight-up business model that respects the rule of law, including state and county property registrars and tax collection systems, along with long-existent land title codes.

The purported electronic mortgage registration system that bypasses state law, MERS, has no place in this world. Nor do complex slice-

and-dice financing models that fed the housing bubble. Like so much of what starts out as a legitimate enterprise, the financial market for these products was turned on its ear and debased to the point that home buyers were duped into being little more than renters. Through the use of ridiculously complex mortgages and their securitization through even more complex instruments, home buyers were effectively forced to serially refinance to keep the gimmicks that allowed them to afford their home. When prices stopped rising, refinancing became impossible, and foreclosures began in earnest.

Those foreclosures laid bare a number of uncomfortable facts. There are now legitimate questions being raised about whether the paperwork necessary to legally transfer mortgages into these securities was ever completed. More than 100,000 foreclosure affidavits had to be withdrawn after the persons attesting to the correctness of information in them admitted that they never read the documents. Lawsuits filed in late 2010 and early 2011 allege that multiple frauds were perpetrated by lenders and securitizers in the packaging and sale of mortgage-related securities.[5]

Many of the problems are traceable directly and indirectly to Fannie Mae and Freddie Mac, if for no other reason than they set forth the structures that were later used in the subprime and ALT-A lending spaces.

Fannie Mae and later Freddie Mac were chartered to provide a reasonable set of services. They abused this trust and were investigated for fraudulent accounting.[6] That investigation did not stop banks from tendering to them bad mortgages that failed to meet their own stated standards, and as of this writing in January 2011, tendering bad loans to the government-sponsored enterprises (GSEs) is still happening.[7] The U.S. dalliance with a broken home mortgage finance system must be terminated and reorganized based on sound fundamentals.

The simplest proposal to reorganize home mortgages is to set up a formal structure under which all home loans are independently graded for characteristics by an accounting board that looks at each loan's actual documentation and assigns it to a pool, with the cost of this determination being assessed by a fixed charge on each loan at origination. Banks that originate loans into these pools will remain fully responsible for any false representation, thus requiring them to perform diligence on each loan that is made. Stripped of the borrower's identity but carrying a unique identification number, it then can be put into securities that are self-extinguishing alongside others with similar objective ratings. Buyers can then purchase these securities, thereby funding the issuance of more loans, and these securities can be registered and traded on national exchanges as a hybrid security, much like a closed-end bond fund does today. Since these securities will trade independently on an exchange, they will be priced by the market every day, just like every other stock. With strong disclosure laws behind these securities, the pool's constituent loans will be visible, along with their specific payment and performance history, allowing analytics to be run on the pools by any interested party. Since these securities will be exchange-traded, there will no longer be any sort of valuation game played by any institution that chooses to hold them. The actual asset valuations behind the loans will be visible to all, and they will be marked to the market nightly at an actual price that a buyer is willing to pay, just like any other stock. Mark-to-fantasy will immediately disappear.

Laurence Kotlikoff, professor of economics at Boston University, has put forward a proposal similar to this that makes sense,[8] retaining Fannie and Freddie in this role. There is no particular reason to argue for or against the institutions that do the collecting and structuring of the notes, but there is reason to be wary of any institution that is not formally accountable to the public. Fannie and Freddie have a long history of hiding behind a claim of sovereign privilege if and when they get caught cooking the books or otherwise misbehaving. But these are details, not principles. Other than the requirement to keep whoever is doing the assembling of mortgages and publishing information on them from being able to hide behind a government shield, Kotlikoff's proposal makes sense.

Banks that wish to offer portfolio lending will be able to do so, and they will be competitive with this system, which will involve only one level of sale. Banks will be able to sell whole loans between themselves, and the unsecured portion, if any, will have to be reserved against. There will be no need for ratings agencies on these transactions since there is nothing to rate, with the market determining the price on any given day just as it does for a stock. The security in question will go away when the last loan is paid off, and the trustee, who will be paid a nominal fee for administering the security and forwarding the monthly dividends and principal payoffs, will be responsible for producing the original mortgage note back to the borrower and recording the release, just as it used to be before the securitization games overtook the housing market in the 2000s.

Since there will be no complex securitization, no dicing and no tranching of loans, there is nothing complicated to record. In the typical transaction, there will be exactly one assignment from the originator of the loan in question to the trust pool. The trust will record the mortgage and take physical custody of the promissory note.

The era of juggling mortgages, liar loans, games played with CDOs and similar financial instruments will permanently come to an end, as will all deposit-based unsecured lending. Banks and other financial institutions that wish to lend on an unsecured basis will have to acquire the capital to be lent from investors, making the risk of default solely theirs. Unsecured lending will become quite expensive, which is exactly as it should be.

■　■　■

No discussion of banking regulation would be complete without addressing derivatives. They are useful and legitimate tools. But their abuse is unacceptable, creates systemic risk where none should exist, and has been repeatedly exploited as justification for government bailouts.

Derivatives act in the economy as insurance policies. Even when used for speculative purposes, the loser of the gamble, when the act insured against occurs, still has to pay off. The premium and payment flow, analyzed objectively, looks an awful lot like an insurance company who wrote the policy on your house that just burned to the ground.

The Commodity Futures Modernization Act must be modified to specify that over-the-counter (OTC) derivatives are per se unlawful gambling constructs. Margin supervision is effectively impossible with OTC derivatives, and there is no reasonable way to ensure that the buyer of such a contract gets a fair price. The usual argument against these requirements is that many of these contracts are so customized in a bespoke fashion as to be impossible to place on an exchange. This argument makes little sense, as a contract that is so highly customized as to be unable to be replicated can also not be reasonably priced in a transparent fashion. While it is true that some of these contracts are indeed highly customized, someone has to take the other side of that risk. In virtually every case, you can deconstruct such a contract into multiple components that are commonly traded and thus can be placed on an exchange. A farmer who is concerned about the price of both oil and wheat might want to enter into some sort of customized agreement, but nothing prohibits him from transacting in the futures market for both wheat and oil. Both of those are regulated markets where transactions are double-blinded and margins enforced.

Beyond price discovery issues, which hurt legitimate producers of goods and services by overcharging them when they desire to buy protection against risk, the problem that arises with asset valuation declines is intractable when the protective instruments are traded over the counter. The practice of chaining contracts exploits intentionally obscured pricing to effectively steal from market participants while creating unnecessary systemic risk. Twenty years of experience and incessant bailouts make clear that the only means available to remove that risk is to prohibit the practice.

When all derivative contracts are double-blinded by an exchange that stands for each buyer as the seller and for each seller as the buyer, systemic risk and price gouging disappears. The exchange, because of its unique standing in the middle of each transaction and fixed compensation for doing so, is compelled to police the ability of market participants to pay. Each party that alleges that it has protection against some event, whether a change in the price of oil or the default of some security, has a reasonable basis for making the claim as opposed to simply saying, "Trust us."

If we had not experienced more than two decades of institutions asserting "trust us" as a general operating principle and then turning around and demanding a bailout from the government, it might be reasonable to accept claims by financial institutions that they can manage these risks on their own. But such an unbroken record does exist, and it has been asserted in each and every case where a large financial institution has gotten itself in trouble, going all the way back to Continental Illinois in the early 1980s. The result has been hundreds of billions of dollars in backstops, and, more important, the behavior that led to each crisis with regard to these instruments has not changed over time.

There is thus no realistic alternative to outlawing OTC derivative trading. Twenty-five years of history says a public exchange mandate for all derivatives is the only way we will find stability in the marketplace and prevent the abuses that in large part led to the financial crisis of 2008. In addition, this proposal fits nicely into the one dollar of capital mandate, in that through robust and public exchanges, there will never be a question of whether a financial institution has the necessary capital behind its positions, should it be called upon to perform.

If a security is too complex to trade on an exchange, then we must ban that security outright. If it's too complex to trade on an exchange where everyone has full transparency with regard to what a security is, how it's priced, and the best bid and offer for that security by a wide range of market participants, then the odds are overwhelming that the complexity is a foil for the purpose of hiding risk. This inevitably leads to someone getting robbed. We have seen repeated examples of these deceptions during the current financial crisis in various structured products, and there appears to be no regulatory solution that will work to resolve the issue, as every regulation that is supposed to protect market participants is simply circumvented with yet another complex product.

Price transparency and market-based valuation for all securities, along with a requirement that lenders use only actual capital for all unsecured lending on a dollar-for-dollar basis, will put a stop to Ponzi-style asset bubbles. Stripped of the ability to create fictional money through the expansion of credit without boundary, those who engage in unsound lending and speculative purchases will bear the full risk and expense when those speculative manias end.

We cannot and should not prevent speculation in the economy, but we can and must end the era of financial interests intentionally creating false views of value, creating credit with nothing behind it other than a bare promise to produce in the future, and fueling bubbles with no actual entity or person known to be able to make good on the bets placed when people come to their senses and the bubble pops.

Chapter 8

Fixing Social Security, Pensions, and Health Care

M uch of what has ailed our economy in the misapplication of leverage has come from various government policies and actions that embed into the economic landscape the desire or even demand for ever-expanding debt. There is an old saying that whatever you provide incentives for, you will get more of, and nowhere is that maxim clearer than in government. To successfully reform our economic system to attenuate the inappropriate abuse of leverage, we therefore must take on the most pervasive of the drivers of this bad behavior, and turn our attention to government programs.

There are no easy answers to the pension, Social Security, and health care issues. The mess we have today has been made by the actions of those who have gone before us, and as a result we have a limited number of options that will actually work. Chief among actions that will not work are pretending that minor tweaks to these systems will save them.

Social Security, according to the 2009 trustee report, has an unfunded liability of about $18 trillion and growing.

But in point of fact, all of Social Security is unfunded.

Ever since the 1983[1] reforms, Social Security and Medicare have taken their tax receipts and paid them into the general fund of the Treasury, receiving in return special Treasury bonds. These are not actual bonds in that they're not marketable. In other words, they're an IOU from Treasury to the Social Security and Medicare funds. This is an accounting fiction since you can spend a given dollar only once. The result of this accounting manipulation is that the federal deficit has looked smaller than it really is since the Social Security tax receipts are spent instead of being put aside.

To spend the IOUs that Social Security has accumulated, the fund will have to take their IOUs to Treasury and redeem them for actual cash. Treasury, having no actual cash since we have run continual budget deficits for decades, will have to immediately issue bonds into the market to redeem the IOUs. For this reason, the Social Security and Medicare accounts should be properly counted as actual federal debt, as that's exactly what they'll turn into the moment the Social Security and Medicare system tries to spend them.

Social Security was not supposed to go into the red—that is, to pay out more than it takes in—until sometime in the 2020s. It also was not supposed to exhaust the IOUs it has received until 2037. But in fact, the program ran an operating deficit in 2010 and will for at least the next two years because of the payroll tax cut that was enacted in the closing days of the 2010 Congress. This will force Treasury to redeem some of those IOUs and issue more real bonds that will directly add to the federal deficit. As the baby boomers retire over the next 20 years, with the largest group retiring during the next decade, payroll taxes will have to increase by more than a third from levels before the cut was made, and by about half again from where the Social Security tax is at present.

The unfortunate fact is that Social Security as it is currently constituted cannot survive. It is part and parcel of the debt-based Ponzi scheme that has been run on the American people, and despite being the third rail of American politics and off-limits to political discourse, we have only two choices. We can deal with the funding problem now, or we will encounter a crisis a few years from now, and certainly within a decade, when we're unable to fund the Social Security checks for retirees.

Public-sector pensions are likewise in serious trouble. Private pensions have an escape hatch for those plans that made unconscionable promises that cannot be kept. If the firm is unable to pay the pensioners and fails, the Pension Benefit Guarantee Corporation (PBGC), a federal agency, steps in. The PBGC then takes over the assets and restructures payments to bring them in line with available financial resources. At present, this forcible restructuring is not permitted for public pensions, some of which have the protection of state constitutional guarantees on payment.

■ ■ ■

To fix Social Security, we must stop pretending that it is a trust fund. The courts, including the U.S. Supreme Court,[2] have ruled that Social Security is a pure entitlement. We must treat Social Security as what it is: a social insurance program that guarantees a minimum amount of income in retirement, funded by today's tax revenues.

It is possible that after getting rid of the pretense that Social Security is a trust or a debt that we will determine that some sort of phase-out of the program is the right thing to do. Alternatively, we might decide to establish a form of actual individual accounts, a true trust arrangement, rather than the chimera we have today. The latter, if we stop using inflation as a means of covering up government deficits and pulling forward demand, would be an effective means of guaranteeing people at least some sort of personal retirement income in their old age.

But this is not Social Security as we know it today.

Public pensions are an even more difficult situation. Today, there are far too many people who game the system, packing their salaries via various schemes to skew the computation of their pension payouts or even retiring and then going back to work for the same municipality, earning both a wage and a pension. This sort of double- and triple-dipping is a serious problem, but even without it, the solvency of these programs could not be maintained, given the promises they've made and the funding the pension systems have available.

These funds must be put under the same restructuring system that private companies go through that cannot meet their pension obligations. The PBGC or a similar agency must be empowered to seize the assets of an underfunded public pension, terminate it for all new participants, and force both an increase in contributions and a reduction in benefits so the fund is actuarially sound. The criteria for such a seizure must be objective and fairly applied across all state and municipal governments. State and local governments that undergo this procedure must be barred from establishing any future plan other than an individual account similar to a 401(k), preventing future abuses. Collapse of a public pension or, worse, the forced collapse of a state or municipal government due to our refusal to deal with chronic pension underfunding is unacceptable. State attorneys general must take a close look at the promises made and fiduciary responsibilities of state and local pension boards to see whether actionable conduct has taken place, and where it has, criminal charges must be brought.

Casting our police and firefighters, along with school employees, out into the cold cannot be allowed to occur. But at the same time, paying $100,000+ pensions to schoolteachers and firefighters on a mass basis is mathematically impossible. These employees did not fund their pensions to this level with their own contributions, nor can we conjure the money out of thin air. Just like all pyramid schemes where the expected rate of return is overstated, the mathematics eventually catch up, and only the early beneficiaries get their money. Instead of allowing a disorderly collapse to take place, we must proactively recast these funds so that everyone who participated receives payouts in proportion to both their contribution and the actual assets in the fund, rather than allowing those who gamed the system or were just lucky enough to be early, to obtain their benefits while everyone else gets nothing.

The loud screaming from public employees, particularly the teachers' unions, is destructive to public discourse and finding a reasonable resolution to this part of the financial crisis. These unions properly had a right of participation in what was sold to their members in terms of the pension plan and its actuarial soundness. If anything, union management is at least as much to blame for these shortfalls as are governments, in that these unions have repeatedly pressed to limit contributions and demand more and more from general tax revenues. While it is certainly true that the state should have been using honest math, the same is true for the union, which had every right and responsibility to act as a watchdog in this process to protect union members.

State, county, and local budgets cannot survive without major and serious reform to these pension systems. If we do not act now, the choices will be forced on us, as those states where the worst abuses took place will find themselves forced to serially raise taxes. But raising taxes drives taxpaying residents away. That spiral, once it begins, is extremely difficult to reverse, and in some areas this mistake has already been made. Every state that has enacted a millionaire's tax has failed to produce the claimed and expected revenue, as those with money move to a lower-tax jurisdiction rather than pay for something they derive no benefit from.

■ ■ ■

Medicare and Medicaid are sometimes referred to as the 900-pound gorilla. In fact, they're more like Godzilla when it comes to economic impact. Medicare alone has nearly $90 trillion in unfunded liabilities. Medicaid, as a pure entitlement program, doesn't have a projected forward deficit, but today it consumes about two-thirds as much revenue as does Medicare. Between the two, they amounted to about 21 percent of all federal expenditures in 2010.

You wouldn't know there was a problem with either from the statements of our last two presidents. George W. Bush added Medicare Part D to the menu, a drug entitlement for senior citizens, and President Obama, in passing his health care reform bill, compounded the errors of everyone before him. The generalized problem with Medicare and Medicaid comes in several forms, as previously discussed, and affects the health care system as a whole. To fix Medicare and Medicaid, we will have to accept a few basic facts, none of which is particularly palatable.

First, we must end differential billing and demand open and transparent pricing for medical procedures, drugs, and devices. This will require that all procedures, drugs, and devices have their prices exposed and be comparable by consumers before service is rendered at all levels, from the local doctor's office to the largest hospital. The local store must post a price and honor it for a television; why should medical providers not have to for a medical procedure? This requirement will immediately bring competition to the fore, and it will end the practice of billing two people wildly different amounts of money for the same thing, predicated only on who or what path payment takes. The same must be true for devices and drugs; a drug that costs $2 a dose must be $2 for everyone, whether you're a cash customer or that amount is billed to an insurance company. Note that this does not prevent you from having some sort of copay, but it does prevent price discrimination for those who choose not to participate in various medical plans.

Second, we must deal with the issue of those who require emergency care but cannot pay, either through insurance or on their own. President Obama's view is that we should all be required to buy health insurance. This is simply an extension of the failed system that has resulted in monstrous medical cost growth for the past 30 years.

We must engage in an honest debate on the issue of unfunded care. EMTALA,[3] the law mandating emergency care for all, must be reexamined and debated in public. The options available to us include either repealing this law and allowing people who choose to be uninsured to bear the risk of medical catastrophe that will go untreated or finding an alternative to forced cost-shifting onto the backs of every other American.

Should we decide as a society that we cannot tolerate letting people who choose to roll the dice with their health care die untreated, we must put in place a system that allows hospitals and other critical care providers such as ambulance companies to bill the government for uncollectible accounts. The government then would act to collect on the bill in question. To fight billing fraud that might otherwise be rampant, this process must contain strong challenge provisions, and there is an argument for handling it through the states rather than at the federal level. By removing the cost shifting that hospitals and other entities currently practice for uninsured and uncollectible accounts, we can keep the mandate that forces treatment in emergencies, and yet the practice of forcing those who can pay, either with insurance or privately, to subsidize those without funds will end. With the imposition of this system, there must also be a means, perhaps through coding on some form of state-issued ID, to specify that a person *explicitly refuses* any such lien and back billing. In the case where that disclaimer is present, no emergency care will be provided if the ability to pay cannot first be ascertained. That in turn will allow those who decide to opt out to choose to take their chances, including the possibility of death, rather than have care and its cost forced on them if they are unable to personally consent. While such a system will not permit collection of all billed amounts, it will place the cost of true indigent and unreimbursed care squarely on the general federal budget, where it can be examined, quantified, and debated.

Along with level pricing and the end of cost shifting, we must figure out how we're going to recover the cost of care for those we cannot collect from because they're here in the United States illegally. Current estimates are that nearly 400,000 children are born to illegal immigrant mothers annually, most uninsured and with insufficient funds to pay for their delivery in cash.[4] If we are going to continue to provide this care to those who are not citizens, then the U.S. government must determine how to collect from these individuals' nation of citizenship. It is manifestly unjust for the U.S. government to foster a flow of illegal immigrants who enter the United States because they can force our citizens to cover their medical expenses. No other nation on earth allows this massive abuse of their taxpayers.

Third, we must reform medical malpractice. There are legitimate malpractice claims, such as when someone goes in for an amputation on their left foot and the right foot is cut off instead. Those victims are due compensation. But much malpractice ends up being defended against prospectively by ordering very expensive procedures and tests, dramatically driving up the cost of routine care. It should be the patient's decision whether to pay for tests to eliminate unlikely but possible diseases and conditions, and the consequence of that decision belongs to the patient. The law must be rewritten to recognize these fundamental choices and lay the consequences for the decisions made on the patient, where it belongs, instead of encouraging and permitting what amounts to a lottery by lawsuit.

Fourth, we must end the practice of defending product pricing across national boundaries. Manufacturers should have the ability to

bring suit or request prosecution to stop counterfeiting but not abro-
gate the common law premise that once you sell something, the person
you sell that item to may do with it as they wish. America cannot
be the land where an erectile dysfunction pill costs $20, while in
Canada the same pill sells for $2. These practices effectively force
everyone in the United States to cover the cost of drug and device
development that then inures to the benefit of everyone else in the
world. We have become forced charitable donors to worldwide health
advancement, and our nation and its people simply cannot afford this
role any longer.

Fifth, we must mandate that if you sell a group plan for insurance,
you must accept all persons under the same plan and with the same
terms. Today, if you work for a large company, insurance is not denied
to you if you are hired and have a preexisting condition. There is no
problem with selling group health plans, whether they are catastrophic
insurance programs or prepaid medical, as is the case with HMOs and
PPOs. If an insurance company is going to do so, however, then these
plans must be open to all on the same terms to bring competition to
the market. If I wish to buy into GM's health plan where I live, I must
be able to even if I don't work for GM, provided I pay the full cost,
including what the employer would otherwise pick up. If insurance
companies want to insist on medical underwriting for a given plan,
they can, but it must apply evenly. The customer can thus choose; it
may be less expensive to buy a plan individually where you're medi-
cally underwritten than to buy into GM's plan, for example, but the
choice should be yours, and the practice of legally discriminating
against those who wish to buy the same product or service from a
given firm must end.

All of these steps will dramatically reduce the cost of medical care.
But even these five steps will not resolve the problem when it comes
to retiree health benefits and care for those who are indigent. Here
we must have a national conversation and debate. Exactly how much
of our tax revenues are we willing to devote to providing health care
for those who are U.S. citizens but cannot pay? Is that number 5
percent of government revenues? 10 percent? 20 percent? There is no
one correct answer, but what we cannot afford to do is write open-
ended checks to everyone in our society, irrespective of need and their

own lifestyle choices. We might want to be able to provide every senior citizen a triple-bypass and two artificial hips, but the money to do so in our tax system simply doesn't exist.

The same circumstance arises for premature births and other extraordinary events. Today, we attempt to save every one of those children, irrespective of cost. Doing so is an admirable goal, but is our society willing to spend what it takes to provide this care? Is that willingness to do so conditioned on how the premature birth came to occur and without regard to the family's resources?

■ ■ ■

There is no one correct answer to these questions, but they are a legitimate part of the public debate. We must not only have that debate but also recognize that how we answer those questions directly feeds into the overall competitiveness of our workforce and people.

This is a debate we have been unwilling to have, as every time the issue is raised, someone starts yelling about how that person is trying to throw Grandma down the stairs. That rhetoric may be useful for scoring political points, but it will not resolve our problems with medical costs. Our technological capability to write checks in this regard dramatically exceeds our society's ability to cash them if we take the provision of free health care for everyone to its logical conclusion.

For this reason, a level-headed debate must be held, and we must determine as a society exactly how much of our domestic output we are willing to tax away and redistribute in the form of care for those who are of modest means and have reached old age or who have insufficient or no resources of their own.

It is fully understandable that those who had promises made to them expect those promises to be kept. But if someone forms a contract with you to jump over the Empire State Building, whether you believe they should be forced to perform doesn't matter. What you contracted to have done is a physical impossibility. These promised benefits cannot be provided. The money does not exist and cannot be conjured into existence, as the premise on which the pledge was made was predicated on phony mathematics and magical thinking.

Chapter 9

Structural Fixes for Trade, Taxation, and Federalism

Ross Perot, during his presidential run in 1992, warned of a "giant sucking sound" coming from the south if the North American Free Trade Agreement (NAFTA) was enacted. He repeatedly claimed that Mexico would drain our industrial base, with factories relocated where labor was available for far less cost than in the United States, and we would all wind up asking, "Would you like fries with that?"

Ross Perot was correct about Mexico, not realizing that China and India were going to do even more damage. The sucking sound of disappearing jobs not only came from the south, it also came from so far west that it was actually in the east!

China and India, between them, have approximately 2.75 billion people. The United States has 330 million.[1] There is no good outcome obtainable by the United States trading on an alleged equal footing with a mercantile China, India, or both. Left alone, companies have shifted their labor abroad and then exported products from China back here to the United States for sale. Beyond the ridiculous trade imbalance this generates and the effective shifting of inflationary pressures to China that should be ours, there is the numerical fact that you cannot raise someone else up that is 10 times your size by allowing them to stand on your shoulders.

Yet we have allowed exactly this dynamic to play out.

There is also the issue of the Chinese currency, the yuan. By pegging their currency to the dollar instead of allowing it to float, our interest-rate environment is effectively pegged to theirs as well, despite the actions of their central bank and the differences in their economy. This is a ruinous problem for both China and the United States. When we run interest rates too low, as we've been doing from 2007 to 2011, the money instantly flows to China via trade imbalances, and they get our inflation whether they like it or not. If China allowed free convertibility and movement of the yuan while retaining their peg, the magnitude of this distortion would be even worse, in that money here would instantly flee overseas to China, where it could earn a greater return.

Unpegging would probably cause China's currency to rise rapidly in value versus the dollar, and that in turn would make their products exported here cost more in terms of dollars. The Chinese don't want this to happen because wage and environmental arbitrage form the core of their ability to export products cheaply to the United States.

The disparities in trade policy don't end with currency imbalances and wage and environmental parity issues. China has a relatively closed market for U.S. products. Many U.S. companies are required to assemble their products and source raw materials from China if they wish to sell their products in Chinese markets. China also frequently imposes joint-ownership requirements on firms, especially for items they consider strategically important to their industry and economy. America does not, in turn, demand the same of Chinese manufacturers that want to sell products into U.S. markets.

Then there are intellectual property issues. China has been implicated in multiple computer break-ins over the last few years, and it is common knowledge within industry that if you have a product manufactured in China, your design will be stolen and duplicated. In the United States, such unfair tactics and outright theft of intellectual property lead to lawsuits, product seizures, and even criminal prosecution. In China, you can pretty much forget about attempting to enforce your rights unless you're Chinese.

India has somewhat more respect for intellectual property, but the same basic issues arise when it comes to wage parity. Their business model is to provide outsourced services to U.S. companies. That's great for the people who get the jobs in India. It's not so great for computer engineers and programmers in the United States who are attempting to compete with someone in India making the equivalent of $30,000. That may be a very nice salary in India, but it is one third to one half of what that job paid 20 years ago in the United States.

■ ■ ■

Fair trade is, in the general sense, a good thing. Beyond the expansion of markets, trading partners have a natural inhibiting factor against aggression, and thus trade helps to maintain world peace. Among developed nations with reasonably similar costs of living, completely open borders when it comes to the passage of goods and services makes good geopolitical and economic sense.

The *CIA World Factbook* estimates the per capita U.S. GDP is 10th in the world, at about $47,000. We compare well with Canada ($46,300), Japan ($42,500), and Sweden ($49,000), among others. But China has a per capita GDP of $4,300, or about 10 percent of our output per person, and India, at $1,200, is literally 2 percent of the United States on a per-person basis.

A $5,000 annual salary in local currency to a person in China is above their per capita GDP. For someone living in India, it's four times the per capita average. But in the United States, you'd starve to death on that total compensation. That salary is about $100 a week, well below the poverty line, and at $2.50 per hour for a standard 2,000-hour person-year, it's also about a third of the minimum legal wage under federal law.

Just as important as wage disparity are environmental issues, as detailed earlier. In China, the level of pollution is legendary, and there are numerous photo essays available on the Web covering the subject. Our rivers used to have poisoned fish in them, and our air was pungent with the smell of chemicals. But we decided in the United States that unsafe water and air was unacceptable, and we forced industry to clean up the land, water, and air. In China and India, that has not occurred, and as a result, it is much cheaper to dump industrial waste into the closest body of water or pollute the air than it is to properly treat it so the environment is preserved. This, of course, makes Chinese or Indian production more competitive.

There is only one realistic way to deal with these labor and environmental issues: Impose wage and environmental parity tariffs, along with a tariff for those nations that manipulate their currency.

Free trade and fair trade are synonyms only when the two nations involved have reasonably comparable standards of living.

Ross Perot raised a stink about Mexico because their per capita GDP was about a quarter of ours. That, he predicted, would lead to heavy manufacturing moving to Mexico and destroying our industrial base. He was right for a while, but what he didn't count on was a drug war that has since erupted in Mexico and trashed its economy and competitiveness, even though plenty of manufacturing did move across the border and drain American jobs.

But the Chinese and Indian problem is even more severe than the issue we have with Mexico. Eventually, those nations will transition to a market economy based on internal consumption. Once that has occurred, free and fair trade will have some congruence, and we will probably be able to trade with both nations without the need to impose tariffs.

But until that time comes, we can only lift those nations up by allowing their people, who outnumber us 10:1, to step on our heads and flatten us into the ground, destroying our nation's standard of living.

The free trade apologists have been beating their drum on this point for more than two decades. They have presided over both parties in Congress and the White House. Their legacy is one of destruction of the standard of living within the United States and environmental devastation in foreign lands, driven by our insatiable desire for cheaper labor. Tariffs are the constitutionally correct means to resolve this imbalance.

■ ■ ■

If trade is a mess, then our tax system is the unholy spawn of Satan. Lucifer himself could write the Internal Revenue Code as it exists today, or something awfully close to it.

There are two basic means by which we can address the intractable problems with taxation in our society. The first is to transition to something akin to a flat tax on incomes, maintaining some degree of progressive rates but eliminating the many-feet-thick Internal Revenue Code with all sorts of social preferences and punishments. A flat tax that replaced all federal income and payroll taxes, including Social Security and Medicare, with a base rate of 10 percent, stepping up to a maximum marginal rate of 30 percent for incomes over $250,000 for a single person, and disallowing all deductions, would result in a tax return that would literally fit on one side of a piece of note-book paper.

Such a tax system could give preference only to long-term capital gains (e.g., a 10 or 15 percent rate for three or five years) and tax corporations doing business in the United States at a singular rate on worldwide income, subject only to an offset for taxes actually paid in another jurisdiction. An alternative would be to not tax corporations at all, recognizing that they simply pass any tax assessed on them through to their customers. At the same time, ending deductions for interest of all forms (including corporate debt) and taxing dividends only for the recipient rather than twice as is done now would remove the incentives for corporate debt accumulation. Since a corporation's stated purpose is to provide benefit to its owners, who are the stock-holders, allowing tax deductibility of interest paid on debt not only incentivizes the accumulation of leverage but also punishes companies that return capital to their stockholders, the very purpose for which corporations are permitted to exist in the first place.

Preventing tax shifting by large corporations would end one of the monstrous advantages that large companies have over small businesses. It is difficult enough to compete against large multinational corporations, given their economies of scale and substantial financial resources, including access to the capital markets that no small business enjoys. When that same corporation is able to employ various legal tax-shifting schemes and pay an effective zero tax rate in the United States, or something close to it, they enjoy an unfair advantage that punishes entrepreneurs who form the job-creation engine of our nation.

The Fair Tax[2] is the other reasonable solution to our tax system that addresses essentially all of the problems we have with the current tax code. It is the only proposal that recognizes that all taxes are paid by people; any attempt to impose a tax elsewhere simply results in that tax being passed through the products and services produced to the consumer or onto a firm's employees. When the product or service is exported, this tax structure results in a tremendous competitive disadvantage to the producer.

The Fair Tax would replace all existing federal income, capital gains, and payroll taxes with a consumption tax on the first retail sale of new products and services. The principle of single taxation at the point of first retail sale would mean that used goods would not be subject to tax at all.

In addition, the Fair Tax would provide a prebate to all documented legal households in the United States in the amount of Fair Tax imposed on a poverty-level income for the people living in that household. The prebate would have the effect of making the amount of money you spend, up to the poverty level, exempt from tax. As this prebate would be paid in advance, there would be no filing of tax returns or claims.

Most businesses today file sales and use tax returns, so there would be little if any additional compliance cost and paperwork within the business community. The states would get a small piece of the collected funds in return for administering the tax for the federal government and remitting funds to it.

A revenue-neutral tax rate has been set at 23 percent inclusive. There are plenty of people who argue that this is dishonest, but they're incorrect. If you get $125 in income and spend the entire $125, the tax is $25 on that purchase and the tax-inclusive rate on your income is 20 percent. Why? You purchased $100 of actual goods and services with $125. That is, as a percentage of the amount of income received, you paid 20 percent of it in tax. If you looked at a register receipt, you might call this a 25 percent tax; that's the tax-*exclusive* rate. But our current income tax system is tax-*inclusive*. You pay tax on your entire income, not on the purchasing power as an addition, so the proper comparison is against the inclusive, not exclusive, rate.

The Fair Tax would involve tearing up the entire IRS code. Doing so would remove tens of billions of dollars of annual expense from U.S. corporations and individuals. The common individual who does not run a business would not need to file or document anything, other than proof of legal residency for everyone in a household to get the prebate. Businesses would get rid of most of their tax compliance costs, leaving only sales and use tax, which they already have, reducing costs dramatically. Illegal aliens would not qualify for the prebate, and as a consequence, we would obtain a simple and natural disincentive to illegal immigration.

Capital gains would be entirely untaxed. The current preference for debt over dividends in corporations would disappear, as neither would be taxed at the time of payment or investment. The production of goods and services and their export would be untaxed as well. America would become an instantaneous corporate tax haven, and thousands of internationally headquartered firms would move here. With these corporation headquarters would come millions of white-collar jobs. Investment would be tremendously incentivized, as there would be no tax on success.

The expression of success via spending, on the other hand, would be a taxable event. If you wanted to buy a new Lamborghini or yacht, you'd pay lots of tax. But if you decided to live in a modest home, your wealth would remain yours and be unmolested.

Additionally, the current black-market economy, including the trade in illegal drugs, results in significant numbers of people who pay no taxes at all. The Fair Tax would eliminate this loophole and expose all these people to taxation, since the illegal drug dealer still buys gasoline, food, electricity, and the other necessities of life.

There are many who argue that the Fair Tax would make the rich richer and disadvantage the middle class and poor. This claim is difficult to defend. At present, individuals pay an effective 15.3 percent tax from the first dollar they earn in the form of Social Security and Medicare payroll taxes.[3] While only half of this tax is visible to you directly, the other half is money you would be paid by your employer if your employer was not required to send it to the government. As such, your offered wage is about 7.5 percent less than it would otherwise be, and under the Fair Tax, that distortion would immediately disappear. If you spent double the federal poverty line in a year, or about $44,100 for a family of four, your effective tax rate would be about 12 percent. Note that the median household income is presently about $49,000, so this compares reasonably well and is in fact less than most people in that tax bracket pay in Social Security and Medicare alone. Many people on the lower end of the economic spectrum would pay less under the Fair Tax than with the current system, but only those living at or below the federal poverty line would get a complete free ride.

The wealthy who wish to live large would pay much more tax than they pay now. None of the current tax shelter techniques used by the rich would provide a safe haven against taxation. If the wealthy decide to invest and risk losing their wealth, they would pay no taxes on that investment until they cash it out and spend it. We must recognize and accept that nobody is ever hired by a poor person. The more actual risk wealthy people take by investing their money in business enterprises, the more jobs we create and the more opportunity we have as a nation. Class warfare is a wonderful political tool, but it makes for terrible economic policy.

One recent argument against the Fair Tax is that governments would pay Fair Tax on their goods and services. This has been claimed to be unfair, but if the purpose is to tax consumption and thus discourage opulence and encourage thrift and investment, it is difficult to understand where the objection comes from. A local jurisdiction that purchases a new police car consumes that vehicle, just as the local city hall does when it buys a computer, laser printer, or ream of paper.

Many wish to drive the acts of the population through tax policy toward or away from various behaviors they want to see either reinforced or curtailed. The Fair Tax eliminates the ability to drive social behavior via taxation. Leaving aside the government's right to influence behavior freely entered into by consenting adults, tax policy is a poor vehicle for expression of this preference and encourages both fraud and economic inefficiency.

The Fair Tax has two other major points to recommend it. Getting rid of the Sixteenth Amendment eliminates the ability to bring an income tax back into the system. It also forces immediate recognition of any future tax increases into the public eye, in that the tax will show up on every register receipt in every store. Given the relatively large and very visible nature of the Fair Tax on every sales receipt, it is reasonable to expect that the public would soon demand a dramatic reduction in the size of the federal government overall.

A full exposition of the Fair Tax is beyond the scope of this book; for more detail, I strongly recommend you read the book of the same name by Boortz and Linder, along with their companion web site (http://fairtax.org).

■   ■   ■

On the spending side, the federal government has a serious problem, and minor changes are not going to cut it. The entitlement system embodied in Medicare, Medicaid, and Social Security cannot be reformed without resolving the problems we have today with federal spending, and our budgetary imbalance must be addressed if we are to ever have a durable and stable economy.

The federal government is allegedly bound by enumerated powers in the Constitution. As just one example of the consequences of the federal government's willful refusal to honor the limits of the Constitution, our present Social Security and Medicare boondoggle would almost certainly not have happened were the programs under state control. Nobody would have tolerated a nonportable retirement or medical program where you paid into a fund and then lost your retirement and medical security if you moved from one state to another. The requirement to provide full portability would have essentially forced the states to actually hold the funds withheld via taxes in trust, rather than raid them as was done by the federal government, so you could take your existing balance with you in those accounts when you moved. In addition, having 50 medical plans competing instead of one gigantic federal institution would have promoted far more competition than we have seen to date.

Banking regulation is properly the purview of the state governments as well, but the Constitution was ignored in 1994 with the passage of the Riegle-Neal Interstate Banking and Branching Efficiency Act.[4] Before that law, along with the Commodity Futures Modernization Act,[5] credit default swaps were regulated as insurance contracts under state law, and the monstrously large banks that now dominate our landscape could have never consolidated to the point of posing the severe systemic risk that arose.

Constitutionally enumerated powers also do not include federal control over education, farm subsidies, or even most of what passes for homeland security, save the portion related to customs and border control. A full list of the usurpations of the Constitution by the federal government is well beyond the scope of this work, but if we are to ever resolve our budgetary issues and dilute corruption in both our government and the broader economy, we must address the proper Constitutional roles of federal, state, and local governments. Doing so will return most of the power of the federal government back to the states. If nothing else, it's much harder to bribe 50 state legislatures and governors with campaign contributions than it is to influence one Congress.

Finally, we must speak about defense spending. It is a common place for people to attack when talking about budget deficits, as defense accounts for some $750 billion a year in federal outlays. What has to be recognized about defense spending, however, is that a huge percentage of Defense Department outlays go toward protecting our access to energy resources. Virtually all of our activity in the Middle East and indirectly in Afghanistan is really about guaranteeing access to oil supplies. Since the 9/11 hijackers were mostly from Saudi Arabia, if we had taken a view toward punishing the responsible parties, we would have hit back at Saudi Arabia immediately. But Saudi Arabia and the related nations in that part of the world sell us about a quarter of our oil imports, and thus we were forced into more of a containment posture. Nigeria and Venezuela are also major exporters to the United States. Among those nations that are stable, only Canada (#1) and Mexico (#3) are reasonably peaceful and have a republican form of government, with Mexico slowly sliding away into drug gang anarchy.

We can and should reduce defense spending, but it is suicidal to cut defense on any large-scale basis until we resolve our nation's energy supply issues. We didn't wind up as the world's policeman out of a desire to be an imperialist. That role came about as a consequence of our need to guarantee access to oil. The irony of this situation is that the political left puts forward both the cutting of defense spending and a pointed refusal to tap and exploit energy sources we have within our nation for environmental reasons, while the political right is interested in both increasing or holding steady defense spending and drilling for oil, but shows little interest in other energy paths. Neither of these political approaches to defense and energy can be viewed as rational. Both paths will ultimately lead to runaway federal deficits, a cutoff of energy resources, war, or perhaps the worst-case scenario: all of the above.

Implementing real structural change to trade and taxation policies will not be easy. Nor will attacking the federal spending monster and neutering it. But even the most cursory glance at our trade imbalance and federal spending growth, the latter of which has doubled in the past 10 years, should make clear that we cannot continue on our present course.

Chapter 10

Devising a Sound Energy Policy

No treatise on the economy is complete without a mention of energy policy, but unfortunately, the United States hasn't had one for the last three decades. Muddle along has been our buzzword for entirely too long, and we simply cannot allow securing our nation's energy needs to remain adrift.

It is impossible in the long run to have economic expansion without energy expansion. To produce 1,000 television sets requires more energy than to produce 100. To produce more automobiles, you require more energy in the assembly plant, the steel mills, and elsewhere. To support a rising population, you require increasing energy resources. Put another way, behind every unit of GDP is a unit of energy output.

It is also a fact that while we have lots of oil in various forms, the inexpensive oil, in terms of both acquisition and processing, has pretty much all been burned up. What's left, and there is a lot of it, is heavy, sour oil and oil-bearing geology such as shale and tar sands.

The simple fact is that petroleum is in everything around you. Every plastic thing in your home or office is made of oil. When you eat, you're eating hydrocarbons, because the fertilizer that was used on the crop is made from natural gas, and without diesel fuel, crops would not be planted, cultivated, harvested, and transported. Beef and other animal products are also dependent on petroleum, as animal feed must be produced for them to eat as well.

We all recognize that oil goes in our fuel tank in the form of diesel or gasoline and that diesel fuel is what much of the Northeast burns for heating purposes in the form of heating oil. Most of the rest of the colder portion of the nation heats with either LPG or natural gas. But few of us think about the irreplaceable part that oil plays in the packaging of everything we buy and its transportation from wherever our goods are made to where we purchase them.

The extraction and processing of oil and natural gas, along with coal, is environmentally disruptive and expensive. So is drilling for offshore oil, and the risks are material, as we discovered with the recent BP spill in the Gulf of Mexico. Nonetheless, our current policy of buying the majority of the petroleum we use from foreign nations, and relying as extensively as we do on those foreign sources, is both economically and geopolitically unsound. The recent unrest in Egypt is a clear warning to the United States in that this disruption could easily spread to major oil-producing nations such as Saudi Arabia, Nigeria, and Venezuela.

Our nation currently spends about three quarters of a trillion dollars a year on defense, or approximately one in five federal government dollars spent. An enormous percentage of that military spending is directly and indirectly related to ensuring that oil continues to flow from places like Saudi Arabia to the United States. Our nation consumes about 7 billion barrels of oil a year and imports roughly half of the total.[1] If we consider that half of our defense spending is required to provide protection for our energy imports, we must add to the economic cost of oil nearly $100 per barrel in the form of military and defense spending above and beyond the current market price. The current economic price of imported oil (as of April 2011) is not $108 but well over $200 per barrel.

■　■　■

Many people are very excited over the new Chevy Volt, claimed to be one of the first all-electric cars. It is, of course, nothing of the sort. GM produced a true all-electric car, the EV-1, from 1996 to 1999. The EV-1 was a commercial failure for the same reason that other pure-electric cars have been and, barring some major technological breakthrough, will be in the future: energy density.

All forms of chemical energy, including oil, are really nothing other than a battery. Oil is nothing more than energy held in chemical form that originated with the sun, and through temperature and pressure in the earth, it has been turned into a somewhat convenient form. When processed into gasoline, it weighs about 6 pounds per gallon and contains approximately 115,000 BTUs, or about 34.8 megajoules per liter of usable energy.

Gasoline engines, along with all other sorts of internal-combustion engines, are quite inefficient. Only about 20 percent of the energy that is in the fuel winds up moving the car. The rest of the energy in the fuel goes out the exhaust pipe or radiator and is wasted. So from the standpoint of the energy in the tank, about 7 megajoules per liter of useful energy propels the car when fueled by gasoline.

Unfortunately, the best batteries we have today, lithium chemistry batteries, are able to reach about 1.3 megajoules per liter of energy density. Electric motors and control systems can be highly efficient—in some cases, able to turn more than 80 percent of the power they consume into useful motion. But even so, the battery-powered car has a huge disadvantage compared with the gasoline vehicle, managing to obtain only about a seventh of the range for the same volume of battery space as a fuel tank. Lithium is also relatively rare as an element in the earth, making it expensive, and it can be dangerous in its own right in that it burns vigorously on contact with water vapor in the air. As a result, accidents where a battery pack splits open can produce very difficult-to-extinguish fires. Finally, there is the matter of charge acceptance. Charging a battery is not 100 percent efficient, and inefficiency in the process causes the battery pack to heat up. This heating limits the speed with which one can recharge the battery in a car, making the five-minute fill-up we enjoy with gasoline impossible.

Those who look toward battery-powered vehicles are going to be disappointed for the foreseeable future. Liquid hydrocarbon fuels are popular not because of a grand conspiracy, as some people claim, but rather because the oxygen necessary for them to produce usable power comes from the air. That oxygen is the lion's share of the mass of the reaction components that combine through oxidation when the fuel is burned in the engine. A battery, which also produces power from a chemical oxidation reaction, must carry its oxygen inside the case, and as a result, it is much larger and heavier for the same amount of energy stored. Further, while a battery is clean in the car itself, the power used to charge the battery has to come from somewhere. Today, most electricity in the United States is generated in coal-fired power plants, yet those who argue for electric cars claim we should not burn fossil fuels. The irony is obvious.

Natural gas, as touted by many, has its place in our energy future. As a fuel, it burns cleanly and produces little other than carbon dioxide and water from its combustion. We have a decent amount of it available in the United States. But using it for light motor vehicles such as cars is difficult, because it does not liquefy at reasonable temperatures and pressures. The use of liquefied natural gas for long-haul trucks can be reasonably implemented but will do nothing for the common consumer's transportation needs. In addition, while natural gas is inexpensive as of the beginning of 2011, it has undergone extreme price volatility over the previous decade. Predicating an energy infrastructure on a commodity with prices at decade lows, when during that decade there have been two spikes to more than three times the current price, is not a prudent course of action, any more than it was prudent to expect oil at under $30 in 2004 to remain permanently inexpensive.

If from this discussion you are led to believe there are no real long-term and stable options available to us when it comes to energy policy, you're incorrect. We have choices we can make in this nation with regard to energy infrastructure and production, and some of them are very promising.

■ ■ ■

One energy option that has gotten little attention is the liquid fluoride thorium reactor (LFTR, pronounced "lifter"). A fluoride salt is used as both the coolant and carrier for the fuel. This is a technology that we built in the 1960s at Oak Ridge National Laboratory after an abortive attempt to find a way to power aircraft with a nuclear power plant.

There are two primary concerns related to peaceful nuclear energy. First is the risk of an accident during operation, which is very real. The U.S. Navy has successfully operated pressurized-water reactors in surface ships and submarines since the launching of the *Nautilus* without ever suffering a radiation-release accident, but our record on land in the commercial realm is not quite as good. Everyone remembers Three Mile Island, although the actual radiation released from the plant was negligible. Fewer remember how close we came to a catastrophic failure at Fermi I, a power-generating and commercially operated but experimental breeder reactor in Monroe, Michigan.[2] Fermi I, using liquid sodium as coolant, a highly volatile metal, lost flow to some of the fuel subassemblies due to an internal heat shield breaking loose and blocking the cooling passages. Physicists at the plant were able to shut down the reactor, but had the internal core melted sufficiently, they would not have been able to do so. The coolant, had it been released, would have spontaneously combusted on contact with the water vapor in the air, leading to a horrific accident, as the coolant had become contaminated and was radioactively hot.

Then there is the Japanese experience with their Fukushima nuclear plant following the earthquake of March 11, 2011. The story of the meltdowns and subsequent impact and cleanup are still being written, but it is clear that there are going to be significant economic impacts in Japan for years and that a substantial release of radioactivity to the environment has occurred. Three operating reactors were scrammed, that is, shut down on an emergency basis during the earthquake without incident. A fourth reactor had recently had its fuel unloaded for maintenance and the spent-fuel pool was thus much hotter than would normally be the case. Unfortunately, the tsunami that followed the earthquake, several meters higher than had been planned for, drowned the on-site emergency generators and destroyed electrical transmission lines coming in from off the site. Conventional nuclear plants cannot reach and maintain a safe cold shutdown without electrical power, and ironically, there appears to have been no plan to ensure that power was available after a natural disaster of this magnitude. Four reactors involved out of six at the site have been economically destroyed, and the fate of the remaining two is in question.

Part of the problem with conventional nuclear power is that using uranium as a fuel requires very difficult isotopic concentration, since only about 0.7 percent of the natural uranium is U-235, the naturally occurring fissile isotope, while most modern power reactor designs require fuel that has 3 to 5 percent fissile content. Because all uranium is the same chemical element, it must be separated by weight, which involves expensive and complicated centrifuge procedures.

Plutonium-239, the other common element used for nuclear power, is not naturally occurring in any material amount. It is produced by nuclear bombardment of the stable U-238 isotope in reactors, which goes through two beta decays to form first neptunium-239 and then plutonium-239. Plutonium-239 is also fissile and thus can be used for power reactors, as can Uranium-235.

Both Uranium-235 and Plutonium-239 are also useful for making nuclear weapons, as both can be induced to go "prompt critical" and explode, as opposed to releasing energy more slowly in a fashion suitable for peaceful power production. In addition, both elements can be handled without the use of heavy shielding, which makes possible the production of nuclear weapons that will not kill anyone that gets in their vicinity by radiation poisoning before they are detonated.

This dual-use feature drove most of the U.S. and other nations' interest in using uranium and plutonium as a nuclear power source, because the same technology used to produce and fuel reactors also yields the material to make nuclear bombs.

Unfortunately, the use of uranium and plutonium for power production creates a significant nuclear waste problem. These reactors produce a large amount of high-level radioactive waste in the form of by-products that are dangerous for thousands of years. While it is possible to reprocess the spent fuel and greatly decrease the amount of waste that must be stored, it is a technically complicated and dangerous process in and of itself, and thus reprocessing is very expensive. Political considerations have also stymied reprocessing in the United States. Fear of nuclear weapons proliferation led Gerald Ford to suspend reprocessing of fuel in 1976, and Jimmy Carter banned it within the United States in April 1977. This ban was officially lifted in 1981 by Ronald Reagan, but the lack of a reasonable regulatory framework has prevented commercial reprocessing from being restarted in the United States.

Today, we are challenged by storage concerns and the fight over exactly where to put all the waste we generate from nuclear power plants. Our present strategy is basically no strategy at all, in that spent fuel is simply stockpiled at plants in cooling pools. The Yucca Mountain facility that was planned as a long-term disposal site has been effectively killed by President Obama and the Senate as of 2009, although House Republicans are attempting to revive its construction. This accumulation of spent but not disposed fuel is dangerous, and yet nuclear waste disposal is a political hot potato that nobody wishes to take on. Nonetheless, this issue must be dealt with, as the accumulation of spent fuel at power plants is an unacceptable risk to both our economy and landscape, should there be a large-scale accident.

To continue or expand the use of conventional nuclear power, there will remain both concerns with waste storage and the means of safely generating sufficient fuel for the reactors themselves via breeders like the one that melted down at Fermi I.

The other easily accessible option for nuclear power, the liquid salt thorium reactor, has far less suitability for weapons use, as the isotope of uranium produced by its operation, U-233, comes with a poison in the form of U-232, which is extremely dangerous to handle due to strong gamma emissions that are products of its decay. This, along with the fact that a thorium-salt reactor breeds fuel relatively slowly as it burns up the original fuel source, makes it difficult and very expensive to use this fuel cycle as a source for nuclear weaponry. For this reason, the thorium fuel cycle has been considered undesirable when nuclear weapons production is part of the overall nuclear infra-structure within a nation.

But for power production, thorium is a nearly ideal, although not yet commercialized, alternative. It breeds fuel and, appropriately managed, also digests most of its own nuclear waste. The resulting nonrecyclable final waste product is both a much smaller quantity and dangerous for a much shorter period of time. This is far different than the tens of thousands of years of isolation necessary with uranium- and plutonium-fueled reactor by-products.

Liquid salt thorium reactors have another advantage over pressurized-water reactors using uranium or plutonium as fuel: They operate at relatively higher temperatures and much lower pressures. The lower pressure makes them safer, as unlike a reactor using pres-surized water as a coolant, there is no risk of a steam explosion in the reactor due to a mechanical failure. The higher temperature of opera-tion, up to 650 degrees Celsius in tested designs, makes the use of process heat—that is, the direct heat from the reactor—practical for a host of industrial uses including processing biological material of various sorts into hydrocarbons for portable energy use. The higher-temperature operation also makes possible the use of extremely efficient turbines for electrical generation that cannot be used with conven-tional nuclear power plants.

In addition, thorium is quite abundant and economically recover-able almost everywhere. One of the places where it is that we'd rather it not be, due to environmental hazard, is in coal. Every 1,000-megawatt electric coal plant produces about 13 tons of thorium a year, contained in the waste ash produced by the plant. The important and overlooked statistic in this fact is that each ton of thorium can produce about 1,000 megawatts of electric energy itself if used as a nuclear fuel. Put more simply, each coal-fired power plant in the United States literally throws away about 13 times as much energy as it produces![3]

Read that again: *We have enough energy necessary to replace all of our current forms of human-consumed energy in the United States for a thousand years, literally sitting in a waste pile, and we throw all of it away.*

This is not pie in the sky technology or a theoretical exercise that we do not yet know how to industrialize. In addition, the inherent safety of this type of reactor has already been proved. Government researchers at Oak Ridge had a reactor running on this very fuel cycle in the 1960s and intentionally left for the weekend on more than one occasion after turning the cooling system off. A freeze plug reached its melting point, and the reactor's working fluid drained out into a holding tank, shutting down the reaction safely with no special pumps, controls, or concerns. On Monday, the coolant was reheated and pumped back into the reactor, which promptly started producing power again.

Should we choose to separate thorium from coal to use it as a nuclear fuel, there is another enticing possibility. The Germans learned how to turn coal into synfuel on a commercial basis out of necessity during World War II, as they had few natural oil resources available to them. This process, called Fischer-Tropsch, has been improved substantially since that time and is used in some parts of the world to provide diesel fuel in locations where there is plenty of coal but little or no oil. Using the processed heat from a thorium-based reactor, we could turn the coal into synthetic fuel compatible with existing diesel and gasoline engines.

Some back-of-the-envelope math discloses interesting facts. We consume roughly 1,100 million short tons of coal annually today, most of it for electrical power generation. We could replace all of our imported oil used for gasoline and diesel fuel while generating more electricity than we get from burning the coal alone and yet not increase our net coal consumption. This would result in a net decrease of CO_2 by the amount of former oil imports that would not take place. Our existing motor vehicles would continue to be viable for personal and business transportation. The elimination of a need to pay for the protection of foreign oil sources would make possible cuts in our defense budget of some $350 billion a year, providing $7 trillion over the next two decades to construct these facilities and a large and permanent federal budget decrease down the road.

■ ■ ■

This is an enticing alternative for our current and future energy needs since we have nearly 500 years of proven coal reserves at existing consumption rates. Even allowing for population growth in the United

States and without expecting any decrease in net energy use by our citizens, this path provides energy independence for more than 200 years and approximately three to five times our current electrical output.

Some research has been restarted on the thorium fuel cycle in the United States in the last couple of years. Much more needs to be done.

Thorium-cycle reactors are not the final answer to our energy concerns, but they are likely to form a part of a sustainable and usable path forward for the United States. A robust scientific and public policy debate about energy has been notably absent in this country for more than 30 years. We must have that debate and discuss how we're going to acquire energy, what ecological and economic costs we are willing to incur to have the energy we need, and what geopolitical risks and force projection we're willing to engage in, given the realities of our chosen energy path. What is certain about our energy future is that if we do not have that debate and begin deploying sustainable technologies that are based on actual science rather than the sort of pie in the sky subsidized models we have toyed with in the past, such as ethanol from corn and direct solar conversion, we will find ourselves both at the mercy of foreign interests and increasingly behind the curve necessary to sustain, much less improve, our way of life.

Resolving these issues and constructing a viable energy policy for our nation is not only an economic imperative but also a geopolitical and social stability must.

Conclusion

The economic crisis that gripped the nation in 2007 was not an accident, and the people responsible not only saw it coming but also knew the crisis would occur. It was inevitable and created by unsound policies at all levels of government and finance. The latest economic upheaval is nothing more than another in a long series of economic catastrophes that stem from fundamental failures to recognize and act on the mathematical realities of finance and rein in abuses of leverage promulgated by the rich and powerful in our society.

None of these issues has been addressed. Dodd-Frank, the recent financial reform law, does not force price transparency on derivatives and contains enough loopholes to drive a Mack truck through. The 2008 emergency bill, EESA/TARP, passed in no small part due to threats of financial Armageddon by both Ben Bernanke of the Federal Reserve and Hank Paulson of Treasury, in fact contained a Trojan horse provision that removed the legal requirement for all bank reserves, allowing banks to create infinite leverage. We have failed to force recognition of losses by the banking industry and have protected various firms from the consequences of their bad lending decisions. By failing to force banks to lend only in a safe and sound manner and to back up their unsecured lending with actual capital, we continue to perpetuate the myth that we can forevermore say, "Charge it" and never pay off the debt we accumulate.

All of these acts have served to hold systemic debt at unsustainable levels rather than allow it to default. As a consequence, our economy remains moribund and employment anemic, despite claimed improvement.

Had our government refused to bail out anyone in 2007 and 2008, the resulting economic contraction would have caused massive bankruptcies and business failures in the banking and industrial portions of our economy. But the political and short-term economic disruption from forcing bad debt into the open argues for, not against, such a course of action. Without correcting the imbalances that exist, we cannot truly have an economic recovery. The distortions we have in our economy today as a consequence of our lack of will continue to compound damage, and when the next systemic shock arrives, we will be forced to face even more economic harm. That systemic shock is certain to arise; we argue only about when, not if, it will occur.

Our trade and tax policies remain broken, and no meaningful changes have been put in place. These policies were a large part of why excessive leverage in U.S. households and industries could be accumulated in the first place. Without correcting trade and tax policies, jobs will not return to the United States, and the labor participation rate, which ultimately drives the ability of the government to fund its programs via taxation, cannot and will not recover on a durable basis.

Finally, our entitlement programs are impossible to fund as currently constituted. Between Social Security, Medicare, Medicaid, unemployment, and general welfare, they consume 56.7 percent of 2010 federal expenditures. Our federal government as of early 2011 is borrowing 43 percent of every dollar it spends. When we add interest on the debt, even if we eliminated every other federal program, including the military, we could not balance the federal budget. We have allowed the entitlement system to grow for too long to make budget reform meaningful without directly reducing those expenditures by very significant amounts. This process by which we have backed ourselves into a budgetary corner at the federal level has been repeated to a large degree in the states as well via their pension and other social service systems, and the impending crisis we face there is an exact duplicate of the unsustainable path we are on within the federal government and the economy as a whole.

The World Economic Forum says that we must issue $100 trillion more in debt[1] over the next 10 years. This requirement is in addition to the doubling we already engaged in on a worldwide basis from roughly $57 trillion to $109 trillion between 2000 and 2009. Does anyone honestly believe that this amount of debt can be taken on and that the interest expense can be paid? Is the premise of being able to continue to double outstanding debt every 10 years forever believable? Against what will this credit be pledged, and how will that debt ever be paid down?

We can no longer afford to play kick the can. The difficult decisions must be made now, and the medicine swallowed, even though it will cause material economic hardship in the short term. If we fail to do so, the mathematics will continue to compound the damage we must absorb until we suffer a collapse in our monetary and economic system, our government, or both.

The math is never wrong.

> The wavelike movement affecting the economic system, the recurrence of periods of boom which are followed by periods of depression, is the unavoidable outcome of the attempts, repeated again and again, to lower the gross market rate of interest by means of credit expansion. There is no means of avoiding the final collapse of a boom brought about by credit expansion. The alternative is only whether the crisis should come sooner as the result of a voluntary abandonment of further credit expansion, or later as a final and total catastrophe of the currency system involved.
>
> —Ludwig von Mises, Human Action, 1949

Notes

Chapter 1, "An Economic Future for America"

1. Bureau of Labor Statistics, Table B-1 series as of March 2011.
2. USDA SNAP Report, Annual Household Participation as of March 31, 2011.
3. Sean Riley, "Treasury May Borrow Federal Retirement Funds in Debt Emergency," *Federal Times*, April 5, 2011, www.federaltimes.com/article/20110405/BENEFITS02/104050306/1001.

Chapter 2, "Principles of Financial Leverage"

1. For more on the tulip mania, read *Extraordinary Popular Delusions and the Madness of Crowds* by Charles Mackay.
2. Public Law 42-131, 17 Stat. 424, often referred to as "the crime of 1873" for its impact on silver prices and mining interests.
3. A significant number of works have been written on or include material related to the Panic of 1873, often referred to as "The Long Depression"; there are too many to cite individually.
4. The National Housing Act of 1938.
5. FDR issued executive orders 6073 and 6102 under the Emergency Banking Relief Act in 1933, which prohibited exporting gold and then confiscating privately held gold under forced conversion to paper money, respectively.
6. Agricultural Adjustment Act, Public Law 73-10, 48 Stat. 31, declared unconstitutional by the U.S. Supreme Court in *United States v. Butler* in 1936.

7. Public Law 73-66, effective June 16, 1933.
8. Federal Reserve Z1 data tables, 1953 to present.
9. Consumer Assistance to Recycle and Save Act (CARS), HR 2751, passed as part of the Supplemental Appropriations Act of 2009.
10. The Emergency Economic Stabilization Act of 2008, PL 110-343, Section 128.
11. S.2856, PL 109-351, signed by President Bush in 2006.

Chapter 3, "The Aughts or the Aught-Not-Haves"

1. Ben S. Bernanke, "Semiannual Monetary Policy Report to Congress," July 18, 2007, www.federalreserve.gov/newsevents/testimony/bernanke20070718a.htm.
2. U.S. Bureau of Economic Analysis (BEA) GDP Series, www.bea.gov.
3. BLS CPI table, ftp://ftp.bls.gov/pub/special.requests/cpi/cpiai.txt.
4. American Community Survey, U.S. Census Bureau, 2000–2007.
5. Price as of February 2011 on "Beyond Talk" plan; market conditions subject to change.
6. All prices as of February 2011; market conditions subject to change.
7. South Dakota's First Premier Bank, first reported on October 15, 2009. A more recent report from February 2011 on money.cnn.com claims the rate is now 59.9 percent. That doesn't change much.
8. 42 USC §1395dd.
9. American College of Emergency Physicians, "The Uninsured: Access to Medical Care," www.acep.org/content.aspx?id=45983.
10. Robinson–Patman Act, U.S. Code Title 15, Section 13.
11. U.S. Census Bureau, Household income series, Table H-8, www.census.gov/hhes/www/income/data/historical/household/index.html.
12. Paul Kanjorski (D-PA), "Mark-to-Market Accounting: Practices and Implications," Subcommittee on Capital Markets hearing in Congress, March 12, 2009.
13. Ibid.
14. The use of IBM as an example is in no way a statement on IBM or its financials but rather is a simple illustration of how option positions work in the marketplace on a commonly held stock.
15. J. R. Vernon, "The 1920–21 Deflation: The Role of Aggregate Supply," *Economic Inquiry* 29 (1991). Estimates ranged from 13 to 18 percent for the actual price contraction over this period.
16. Ben Bernanke, CNBC, January 13, 2011, 2:40 P.M., "Small Business Forum" panel coverage in an interview with Steve Liesman.
17. U.S. Treasury, "Debt to the Penny." The Bush deficits were approximately $600 billion annually from 2003 to 2007; the 2008–2010 calendar years measured $1.470, $1.612, and $1.714 trillion, respectively.
18. Federal Reserve Z1, March 10, 2011, table Z1/Z1/LA794104005.Q.

19. U.S. Constitution, Article I, Section 10: "No State shall . . . emit Bills of Credit."
20. Federal Reserve Z1, December 9, 2010.

Chapter 4, "The Failure of Kicking the Can"

1. Washington Mutual Quarterly Report, first quarter 2007, http://edgar.sec .gov/Archives/edgar/data/933136/000115752307003679/a5377269ex991 .htm and http://market-ticker.org/akcs-www?singlepost=2137540.
2. Henry Paulson, *CNN Late Edition*, referenced July 21, 2008, by CNBC, www .cnbc.com/id/25764545/Paulson_U_S_Banking_System_Fundamentally _Sound.
3. *The Market Ticker*, "But It Was All Borrowers!" http://market-ticker.org/ akcs-www?post=177288 and Janet Tavakoli, "Blame the Victims and Enrich the Perpetrators," *The Huffington Post*, January 13, 2011, www.huffingtonpost .com/janet-tavakoli/third-world-america-blame_b_808592.html.
4. ACA sues Goldman Sachs alleging fraud, Case 650027/2011, NY State Supreme Court.
5. William Heisel and Ralph Vartabedian, "Regulator Provided Cover for IndyMac," *Los Angeles Times*, December 23, 2008, http://articles.latimes .com/2008/dec/23/business/fi-indymac23.
6. William K. Black, "When Fragile Becomes Friable: Endemic Control Fraud as a Cause of Economic Stagnation and Collapse," in *White Collar Crimes: A Debate*, ed. K. Naga Srivalli (Hyderabad, India: ICFAI University Press, 2007), 162–178; and William K. Black, *The Best Way to Rob a Bank Is to Own One* (Austin: University of Texas Press, 2005).
7. Paul Kanjorski (D-PA), "Mark-to-Market Accounting: Practices and Implications," Subcommittee on Capital Markets hearing in Congress, March 12, 2009.
8. Federal Reserve Z1, December 9, 2010.
9. Blake Ellis, "Home Values Tumble $1.7 Trillion in 2010," *CNN Money*, December 9, 2010, http://money.cnn.com/2010/12/09/real_estate/home _value/index.htm.
10. Ben S. Bernanke, "Deflation: Making Sure 'It' Doesn't Happen Here," Speech, November 21, 2002, www.federalreserve.gov/boarddocs/speeches/2002/ 20021121/default.htm.
11. Representative Brad Sherman, October 2, 2008, on the floor of the House, in which he stated that members were told there would be martial law, www .youtube.com/watch?v=gnbNm6hoBXc.

Chapter 5, "The Folly of Avoidance"

1. Federal Reserve Z1.
2. Treasury Borrowing Advisory Committee, February 2011 Report, p. 23, www .treasury.gov/press-center/press-releases/Documents/TBAC%20Discussion %20Charts%20Merged%202.2011.pdf.

Chapter 6, "Reinstating the Rule of Law"

1. Richard M. Bowen, sworn testimony before the Financial Crisis Inquiry Commission, April 7, 2010, http://fcic-static.law.stanford.edu/cdn_media/fcic-docs/2010-04-07%20Richard%20Bowen%20Written%20Testimony.pdf.
2. Michael Smith, "Banks Financing Mexico Gangs Admitted in Wells Fargo Deal," *Bloomberg News*, June 28, 2010, www.bloomberg.com/news/2010-06-29/banks-financing-mexico-s-drug-cartels-admitted-in-wells-fargo-s-u-s-deal.html.
3. Carrick Mollenkamp, "Probe Circles Globe to Find Dirty Money," *Wall Street Journal*, September 3, 2010, http://online.wsj.com/article/SB10001424052748703431604575468094090700862.html.
4. Martin Z. Braun and William Selway, "State Finances Rigged in Conspiracy by Banks, Advisers," *Bloomberg News*, May 18, 2010.
5. Black, *The Best Way To Rob a Bank*.
6. United States Code: Title 12, Chapter 16, Section 1831o.
7. Anton Valukas, "Lehman Brothers Holdings Inc. Chapter 11 Proceedings Examiner's Report," *Jenner & Block*, http://lehmanreport.jenner.com/.

Chapter 7, "Reforming the Fed, Lending, and Derivatives"

1. 12 USC §225a, www.federalreserve.gov/aboutthefed/section2a.htm.
2. Formerly U.S. Code Title 18, Part 1, Chapter 17, Sec 331, modified in the 1940s.
3. Dennis Kucinich, HR-6550, "National Emergency Employment Defense Act of 2010," December 17, 2010.
4. U.S. Code Title 12, Section 1831o.
5. *Dexia Holdings et al. v. Countrywide Financial et al.*, filed January 24, 2011, and *Allstate Insurance Co. v. Countrywide Financial Corp.*, 10-CV-9591, U.S. District Court, Southern District of New York.
6. Kathleen Day, "Study Finds 'Extensive' Fraud at Fannie Mae," *Washington Post*, May 24, 2006.
7. Bob Ivry and Bradley Keoun, "Citigroup 45% Gain Masks Flawed Mortgages Freddie Mac Calls Not Acceptable," *Bloomberg News*, January 18, 2011.
8. Laurence Kotlikoff, "Turn Them into Mortgage Mutual Fund Companies," *Economist*, July 16, 2010.

Chapter 8, "Fixing Social Security, Pensions, and Health Care"

1. Formally, "The National Commission on Social Security Reform" (NCSSR), chaired by Alan Greenspan and impaneled by President Reagan.
2. *Fleming v. Nestor*, U.S. Supreme Court, 363 U.S. 603 (1960).
3. 42 USC §1395dd.

4. Steven A. Camarota, "Births to Immigrants in America, 1970 to 2002," *Center for Immigration Studies*, July 2005, http://cis.org/ImmigrantsBirths-1970-2002.

Chapter 9, "Structural Fixes for Trade, Taxation, and Federalism"

1. *CIA Factbook*, https://www.cia.gov/library/publications/the-world-factbook/geos/us.html.
2. H.R. 25, *The Fair Tax Act of 2011*, 51 cosponsors.
3. The lame-duck session of Congress in 2010 reduced the employee portion of FICA to 4.2 percent for two years; as of January 2011 the combined payroll tax rate is 13.3 percent.
4. Public Law No. 103-328, 108 Stat. 2338.
5. The Commodity Futures Modernization Act of 2000, originally HR 5660, 106th Congress, 2nd session.

Chapter 10, "Devising a Sound Energy Policy"

1. U.S. Department of Energy, www.eia.doe.gov/energyexplained/index.cfm?page=oil_home#tab2.
2. The author's next-door neighbor was a physicist at the plant; multiple books, some of dubious technical accuracy, have been written about the accident, including "*We Almost Lost Detroit*."
3. Calculation based on approximately 500 tons of coal consumed per hour in the aforementioned 1,000 megawatt-electric plant and the abundance of thorium found in coal per the USGS (http://pubs.usgs.gov/fs/1997/fs163-97/FS-163-97.html); these figures are reasonably conservative with some resources claiming coal burn rates of nearly double that per-hour tonnage.

Conclusion

1. World Economic Forum release, Davos Meeting, *Telegraph*, January 18, 2011, www.telegraph.co.uk/finance/financetopics/davos/8267768/World-needs-100-trillion-more-credit-says-World-Economic-Forum.html.

About the Author

Karl Denninger is an entrepreneur who founded and was CEO of Macro Computer Solutions, Inc. (MCSNet) in the 1990s, one of the first firms to bring the Internet to the greater Chicago area. His background includes corporate management, data networking, and computer engineering. Having worked in firms large and small, from the two-man shop to the Fortune 50, he has nearly three decades of experience. He was one of the few to sound the alarm in 1999 on the impending Nasdaq stock market collapse, after he successfully negotiated the sale of MCSNet to Winstar Communications in the summer of 1998.

Denninger has been an independent trader and financial analyst since 1998 and publishes the popular web periodical *The Market Ticker*. He received the 2008 Reed Irvine Accuracy In Media Award for Grassroots Journalism for his coverage of the 2008 market meltdown.

Index

204 INDEX

Spending (*continued*)
  federal government, 169–170
  IOUs of Social Security, 152
  mandatory, 26
  stimulus, 91
  universities and, 55
Stable prices, 112–114, 137–138
Stafford student loan, 56
Stimulus spending, 91
Stock bubble, of 1990s, 62
Stock market. *See also* Stock prices
  collapse during 2007–2009, 61, 98
  corporate leverage and, 68
  investing in, 92
  in 1987, 72
  in 1929, 16, 17
  in 1920–1921, 77
  in 2008, 80
  in 2000–2010, 92
Stock prices. *See also* Stock market
  acceleration of, 85–86
  Fisher on recession in, 17
  gains on long-term basis, 64–65
  intangibles and, 61
  from 1953–1991, 61–62
Strike price, 69
Strikes, of railroad labor unions in 1877,
    15
Student loan programs, 55–56, 57–58

Tangible assets, 62, 107
Tariff, 165
TARP bill of 2008. *See* Troubled assets
    relief program (TARP) bill of
    2008
Tax, Fair. *See* Fair Tax
Taxes:
  budget gap and, 126
  payroll, fair tax and, 166
Tax-exclusive, 167
Tax-inclusive, 167
Tax system, 8, 165–171
Technological revolution, 37–38

Technology, deflation in economy and,
    113–114
Technology stocks, collapse of, 116
*The Best Way to Rob a Bank Is to Own
    One* (Black), 129
Third Reich, 126
3/27 subprime mortgage, 44
Trade, fair, 163–165
Trade, free. *See* Trade, fair
Trade and tax policy, 161–171, 184
Trade learning, 48–59
Trade *vs.* college education, 58–59
Treasury Primary Dealer network, 99
Troubled assets relief program (TARP)
    bill of 2008, 34
Tulip mania in Holland, 14
2008:
  global market meltdown in, 68
  Paulson on banking system, 96
2011:
  dividends, 64
  federal debt, 6, 124
  manufacturing employment, 5
2009:
  debt-adjusted growth, 84
  stock market in, 100
2001, people with jobs, 106
2007:
  collapse of Bear Stearns hedge funds,
    96
  economic damage in, 85, 183
  leverage in, 108
  mortgages purchased and sold in,
    128
2007–2009:
  collapse of stock market, 61, 98
  financial panic of, 4
2007–2011, low interest rates in, 162
2007–2010, 130
2006:
  Home prices in, 95–96
  mortgages purchased and sold in,
    128